Tim —
Always & forever

9-1-87

# Clippers of the
Port of Portsmouth
*and the men who built them*

Published in cooperation with
Port of Portsmouth
Maritime Museum

# *Clippers of the Port of Portsmouth*
## *and the men who built them*
### *by Ray Brighton*

PORTSMOUTH MARINE SOCIETY
Publication Five

Published for the Society by
Peter E. Randall
PUBLISHER

© 1985 by The Portsmouth Marine Society
Printed in the United States of America
Designed and produced by Peter E. Randall Publisher

*Jacket:* **Morning Light** *entering San Francisco Bay. Painting by John Stobart.*

*A publication of the*
 *Portsmouth Marine Society*
 *Box 147, Portsmouth, NH 03801*

*Other Portsmouth Marine Society Publications:*
 1. *John Haley Bellamy, Carver of Eagles*
 2. *The Prescott Story*
 3. *The Piscataqua Gundalow,*
   *Workhorse for a Tidal Basin Empire*
 4. *The Checkered Career of Tobias Lear*
 6. *Portsmouth-Built*
   *Submarines of the Portsmouth Naval Shipyard*
 7. *Atlantic Heights*
   *A World War I Shipbuilders' Community*

**Library of Congress Cataloging in Publication Data**

Brighton, Ray.
 Clipper ships from the port of Portsmouth and the men who built them.

 (Publication / Portsmouth Marine Society ; 5)
 Bibliography: p.
 Includes index.
 1. Clipper-ships—New Hampshire—Portsmouth. 2. Ship-building—New Hampshire—Portsmouth. 3. Navigation—New Hampshire—Portsmouth. 4. Portsmouth (N.H.)—History, Naval. I. Title. II. Series: Publication (Portsmouth Marine Society) ; 5.
VK25.P67B75   1985       623.8'224'09426       84-18128
ISBN 0-915819-05-8 (hard)

# Contents

|      |                                  |     |
|------|----------------------------------|-----|
|      | Illustrations                    | 7   |
|      | Acknowledgments                  | 9   |
| I    | The Golden Days of the Clippers  | 11  |
| II   | George Raynes & Son              | 16  |
|      | *William E. Roman*               | 23  |
|      | *Sea Serpent*                    | 27  |
|      | *Wild Pigeon*                    | 32  |
|      | *Witch of the Wave*              | 39  |
|      | *Tinqua*                         | 46  |
|      | *Emily Farnum*                   | 59  |
|      | *Witch of the Wave (II)*         | 63  |
|      | *Shooting Star (II)*             | 65  |
| III  | Fernald & Petigrew               | 67  |
|      | *Typhoon*                        | 70  |
|      | *Red Rover*                      | 78  |
|      | *Water Witch*                    | 85  |
|      | *Dashing Wave*                   | 88  |
|      | *Express*                        | 96  |
|      | *Midnight*                       | 100 |
|      | *Noonday*                        | 103 |
| IV   | Tobey & Littlefield              | 106 |
|      | *Morning Light*                  | 108 |
|      | *Sierra Nevada*                  | 115 |
|      | *Ocean Rover*                    | 120 |

| | | |
|---|---|---|
| V | The Hanscoms | 122 |
| | *Nightingale* | 127 |
| | *Josephine* | 134 |
| VI | The Badgers | 136 |
| | *Fleetwood* | 143 |
| | *Granite State* | 145 |
| | *Cathedral* | 146 |
| VII | Daniel Moulton | 150 |
| | *Morning Glory* | 152 |
| | *Star of Hope* | 154 |
| VIII | The Pierces | 156 |
| | *Charger* | 158 |
| Notes | | 162 |
| Bibliography | | 168 |
| Index | | 170 |

# *Illustrations*

| | |
|---|---:|
| *Ocean Rover*, sailing card | 10 |
| Portrait of George Raynes | 17 |
| Raynes tombstone | 22 |
| *Sea Serpent* passing South Head, San Francisco, painting | 26 |
| *Wild Pigeon* under sail, painting | 33 |
| Portrait of Captain Hanson | 35 |
| *Witch of the Wave* in rough seas, painting | 38 |
| *Witch of the Wave*, drawing by F. Della Motte | 41 |
| *Witch of the Wave*, in Boston Harbor, magazine illustration | 43 |
| *Tinqua* off Hong Kong, painting | 47 |
| *Wild Duck* in stormy seas, painting | 51 |
| *Coeur de Lion* leaving port, painting | 55 |
| *Emily Farnum*, a half model | 60 |
| Fernald family tombstone | 69 |
| *Typhoon* off Liverpool, England, painting | 71 |
| *Red Rover* off Holyhead, painting | 79 |
| *Red Rover* renamed *Young Australia*, photograph | 82 |
| *Water Witch* at sea, painting | 84 |
| *Dashing Wave* entering Boston Harbor, painting | 89 |
| *Dashing Wave* under sail off San Francisco, photograph | 94 |
| *Dashing Wave* stripped down as a barge, photograph | 95 |
| *Midnight* on stormy seas, painting | 101 |
| *Midnight* in port, painting | 102 |
| *Noonday* bell, recovered from the ocean in 1934, photograph | 105 |
| *Morning Light* under sail, painting | 109 |
| *Sierra Nevada* heading towards port, painting | 114 |
| *Sierra Nevada* renamed *Royal Dane*, under the Union Jack | 118 |
| *Nightingale*, sailing card | 126 |
| *Nightingale* getting under weigh off New York, painting | 128 |
| Portrait of Samuel Badger | 137 |
| Badger tombstone | 140 |
| *Star of Hope* on the beach near the Cape of Good Hope, photograph | 155 |
| *Charger* sailing card | 159 |

# Acknowledgments

As IS ALWAYS THE CASE in completing a work of this nature, there are many people to be thanked for their assistance and encouragement. Without Joe Sawtelle's persistent urging, it would not have been written, and without his work in the archives of many marine museums much of the material would still remain in those dusty repositories. Further, no book about Piscataqua clippers is possible without reference to the work of the late Gertrude Pickett. Through family ties, Mrs. Pickett had access to the Fernald & Petigrew papers, and made much use of them in her book, *Portsmouth's Heyday in Shipbuilding*. Librarians by the dozen should be individually thanked, but that is impossible, and it is hoped that they understand. Two friends in Kittery, William E. Dennett and Leon French, Jr., directed the author's erring steps when he was searching out the Badgers. Peter Randall offered frequent advice, solace, and exercised his photographic talents to general benefit. And, once again the author had the copy-reading help of Betty J. Nelson in spotting some of the more glaring errors before the book was turned over to copy editor Elizabeth Knies, from whom came many helpful suggestions.

*Clippers of the Port of Portsmouth and the Men who built Them* was fun to do. Much of the basic research was done more than 30 years ago with little thought that it would finally see public print. But Piscataqua shipwrights contributed far more in the past three centuries than twenty-eight clipper ships. Literally hundreds of three-masted, square-rigged vessels have been floated on the Piscataqua, and it is hoped that the stories of many of them will be told in later volumes.

Capt. Charles F. Briard was ready to take Ocean Rover to sea as this sailing card proclaims. Sailing cards were used by ship owners to promote passages on upcoming voyages. Bostonian Society, Boston, collection.

# I  *The Golden Days of the Clippers*

FIRST IT SHOULD BE UNDERSTOOD that if the clipper concept in sailing ship design had not already been conceived, it would have been in the 1850s. A wise man once wrote: "Necessity is the mother of invention," and so it was with American clipper ships. Their time was brief, but they met the contemporary demand for speedier methods of transportation. For easy comprehension of the forces that brought the clippers into being, a modern parallel will serve well. Since World War II millions of traveling Americans have demanded faster and better service across the oceans and the continent itself. To meet this need the airlines have purchased wide-bodied jet aircraft — 747s and DC-10s — and the real clippers of jet flight, the supersonic transports.

So it was with the American clipper, descending in logical progression from sharply built privateers and slavers demanded by the mariners of the early nineteenth century. Those millions of ship lovers who have thronged to see the "Tall Ships" sail into East Coast ports in recent years have caught an inkling of the majesty of a clipper under full sail. But only an inkling, because there have been no clipper ships for a hundred years, at least not in the Piscataqua. An item that appeared in *The Portsmouth Chronicle,* December 1, 1885, confirms this:

> It is many years since a merchant ship, a genuine square-rigger, fully laden, arrived at this port; just how many we cannot say, but we think it must be 25 or 30 at least. If we remember aright, the ship *Simla* was the last one to come up the Piscataqua, this is not far from 20 years ago, but she brought no cargo, her errand being to go into the naval dry dock for repairs [May, 1866].[1] The *William H. Marcy* was the last merchant ship to sail from this

11

port [July, 1875], we believe, but she has never returned, and never will, having been sold some time ago [February, 1882], to go under a foreign flag.

The clipper concept in ship design was nearly a century old when it suddenly came into full bloom in the 1850s. In the early years of colonial America, the design of three-masted, square rigged vessels changed very little. The *Mayflower II*, riding at her berth in Plymouth, Massachusetts, well illustrates the type of ship that made the "Great Crossing" in the sixteenth, seventeenth and early eighteenth centuries. High forecastles and soaring poop decks made them lumbering arks. As the eighteenth century wore along, modifications were made in their design. For example, the Piscataqua-built *HBM America* (1749), had much lower peaks, fore and aft, as a model in the Portsmouth Athenaeum clearly shows. The bows of such ships were like blunt mauls, but changes were coming. They could carry a lot of cargo, but it took them a long time to do it. Boston's Judge Samuel Sewall, late in 1688, made what was a speed run when the ship he was on took only fifty-two days to make the passage to England. Crossings of two months or more were common. The judge did even better on his return passage which took only fifty days. A century after Judge Sewall's journey, Portsmouth-born Tobias Lear crossed from New York to Glasgow in twenty-eight days, at about the same time of year, so perhaps Lear's transport was a better designed vessel.

The period of the American Revolution saw the introduction of a vessel design which became known as the Baltimore Clipper, named for the port in which it was first built. These vessels, with their lean, rakish hull design and fore and aft-rigged sails, were schooners. They played a part as privateers in the War for Independence. A noted authority, the late Howard I. Chapelle, wrote:

> It would be impossible to write a history of American privateering, the slave trade, or even of piracy without mention of this type of vessel. The "rakish topsail schooner" is so often mentioned in the voyage of the mariners of the early 19th Century, that one's curiosity cannot but be aroused as to the history and appearance of these craft. Generally schooner-rigged, they were often engaged in illegal trades—in smuggling in the West Indies and in piracy...
>
> The chief characteristics of these craft were long, light, and extremely raking masts; very little rigging, low freeboard, great rake to stem and stern posts ... Nearly always flush-decked, they had wide clear decks, suitable for working ships and handling the guns.[2]

Vessels with this type of rigging and hull design were familiar to mariners along the East Coast. One of the first of the Baltimore-clipper type known to have come into Portsmouth Harbor early in the War of 1812, was the privateer *Fox*. The *Fox* was built in Portland for the express purpose of privateering and could have carried sixteen carriage guns.[3] When she first came into Portsmouth in September, 1812, she mounted twelve carriage guns and two swivels with a crew of eighty-five. The *Fox* was enormously successful in achieving the purpose for which she was built, taking seven prizes worth half a million dollars. Yet, when the war was over, and no one felt any need for a vessel of her lean design, she was sold for $2,400 and turned into a freighter. It was later said she was so rakish that her cargo was often wet. That complaint was a major factor in the slow acceptance of the clipper style. Old salts simply did not think the design was practical. How many of the men who would later build Piscataqua clippers ever saw the *Fox* is not known. It is probable that Samuel Badger did see her, and George Raynes might have, as they were then teen-agers, but the others would have been far too young. When the clipper builders were learning the shipbuilding trade, their shop talk must have been about the sleek vessels that could cut through the waves faster than any other craft. But acceptance came reluctantly:

> The first ship, called large, to be built on these lines, was the *Ann McKim*, 494 tons, launched in Baltimore in 1833. In her prime she was considered the fastest merchant ship afloat. The *Rainbow*, built in New York in 1845, was the second. The success of these two led to others being constructed of sharp model, principally for use in the China trade.[4]

Interest in clippers built up slowly, and did not reach full spate until after the discovery of gold in California in 1848. The madness brought by gold fever spurred the building of faster and faster, and bigger and bigger, ships. Although would-be miners often went to the West Coast in them, the main urgency was to transport goods to the boom town of San Francisco where they would sell at high prices. Two statistical notes are illustrative: in 1849, there were only fifty-eight ship arrivals in San Francisco; in 1850, by the end of July, there had been 493. Imaginative merchants had already begun buying clippers for the purpose of the tea trade to China, but now it made even more sense to have their ships load for California, unload in San Francisco, then sail across the Pacific to the tea and silk markets in India and China, thence home by way of the Cape of Good Hope. That meant profits both coming and going.

Small vessels like the 500-ton *Martha*, built by Samuel Badger in 1843, simply weren't the answer. The *Martha* was the first to leave Portsmouth with a shipload of forty-niners, bound around Cape Horn. It took the valiant *Martha* 208 days to reach San Francisco.

It was obvious that the *Martha*s of the ocean world couldn't meet the mounting demand. So what could? While the gold fever raged, the clippers provided an answer. They enjoyed a vogue that reached a climax within six years of the laying of the first clipper keel on the Piscataqua, and saw the launching of the last one before the end of the 1850s. That first Piscataqua clipper was the *William E. Roman*; before it went out of business, the George Raynes Shipyard built the first and some of the fastest, and the last Piscataqua clipper. Right in the thick of it with George Raynes were brilliant builders like Frederick W. Fernald and William Petigrew, Stephen Tobey and Daniel Littlefield, Samuel Badger, Samuel Hanscom, Daniel Moulton and Elbridge G. Pierce.

No expense was spared in making these clippers the most ornate marine creations ever built for merchandising purposes. When the clipper era was nearing its peak in 1853, *The Portsmouth Chronicle* published an analysis of the cost of building ships of more than a thousand tons in the various northeastern shipbuilding districts. In New York and Boston the cost was $62 per ton. Surprisingly, the Piscataqua district was right up there with the metropolitan centers—$62 a ton. Perhaps it was the high order of workmanship that brought New York and Boston shipping firms to the Piscataqua for their vessels. Better buys could be had in Maine at $50 a ton, and in New Brunswick at $45. "The naked cost of a thousand-ton ship, first class, in New York, without the ornaments so freely lavished on them, is $62,000."[5]

*The Chronicle* apparently was startled right out of its ink pot when it reported on March 4, 1853, that ship carpenters were in such demand that they were getting two dollars a day. It must have startled Samuel Badger, too, because when he was building ships in the late 1830s and early 1840s that was what he was charging customers for his own efforts as master shipwright. And the two dollar level should not have been all that surprising. In October, 1850, carpenters building the Navy Yard's new floating dry dock on Pierce Island, along with their colleagues in one of the private yards, staged a strike for higher wages, asking $1.75 for first-class journeymen; $1.50 for second-class; and $1.25 for all others. The strike failed because the desire for clippers had not yet reached fever pitch.[6] But, as *The Chronicle* noted, the demand for the skilled artisans needed to create these glamorous ships drove wages up.

The construction of expensive passenger facilities was justified because there was demand for them, just as there are travelers today who will not settle for less than a lounge chair on an SST to Paris. Passengers in the 1850s, embarking on the *Sea Serpent*, one of the fastest clippers, would be calling the ship home for three to four months, depending on the whims of the wind and tide and the skills of her crew. Travelers by clipper needed comforts to offset the long and often hazardous passages.

Of the more than 200 clippers built in the United States, twenty-eight came from the Piscataqua, and some attained fame of far-reaching dimensions. One such was the *Nightingale*, believed to have been the most expensively appointed vessel ever launched on the river.

Ironically, NONE of the clippers built on the Piscataqua ever returned to the river. Today, Piscataqua Valley people cherish the memory of those fantastic ships, but not one clipper built here ever entered Portsmouth Harbor again. Many of them went out of the river under tow by the *R. B. Forbes*, a steam tug sent by Boston and New York ship owners to haul their new vessels to a place where they could be rigged and decorated according to the whims of the time. In fact, only two of the twenty-eight clippers built on the Piscataqua sailed from Portsmouth Harbor on commercial passages. Many of the clippers were owned, at least in part, by Piscataqua investors, but they were leased out to big shipping concerns in New York and Boston. Why? The Greater Portsmouth Chamber of Commerce and the New Hampshire Port Authority are still confronting the issue. Yet the answer is simple: there is not a productive hinterland! There's little or nothing for freighters to take out! In the 1980s, ships come in and load up on rusted-out motor vehicles, and then head for the steel mills of Japan, but that's almost the limit of outgoing cargo.

Through the middle years of the nineteenth century, square-rigged vessels, fully rated as ships, did bring cargoes to Portsmouth. Often the freight consisted of salt, as it still does today. Now the salt is used on the ice-slicked highways in winter, but in other days it was used to salt the fish that was once a major project for shippers on the river. But those ships were not clippers.

It should not be thought, however, that the phasing out of clippers brought an end to commercial shipbuilding on the Piscataqua, because that is not so. Major vessels, such as the earlier mentioned *Simla*, were launched, and one of the greatest promoters of Piscataqua shipbuilding was one of Portsmouth's least appreciated citizens — Daniel Marcy. Perhaps in another volume more tribute can be paid to Daniel Marcy, a captain who took more ships out of Portsmouth Harbor on maiden passages than any other, though not one was a clipper.

When the days of the clippers were booming, Portsmouth people, and those in other Piscataqua communities, experienced an excitement never again equalled. There was a pride in craftsmanship reflected in *The Chronicle*'s obituary of Samuel L. Fernald of Eliot, who died at the age of seventy-three:

> ...Thus are passing away the old-time ship carpenters on the Piscataqua, of whom there has scarcely been the like before, and perhaps may never be the like again.[7]

# II  George Raynes & Son

IN PORTSMOUTH, NEW HAMPSHIRE, today only a stub of a street and a tall granite shaft in Union Cemetery are reminders of one of the greatest craftsmen ever to practice the ship-building trade in the city. Appropriately, Raynes Avenue, which bounds the north edge of *The Portsmouth Herald* property on Maplewood Avenue, runs across the site of the one-time Raynes Shipyard, and Raynes's tombstone overlooks the place where his building ways once stood. For some unfathomable reason Raynes's fame is confined to the Piscataqua, while that of Donald McKay, the New York shipbuilder, is universal among clipper ship admirers. Mention Donald McKay, and many can conjure up the image of the *Flying Cloud*. But that's not so with George Raynes. Yet the man was every bit as much a ship-building genius as McKay. The cause may stem from the fact that McKay practiced his craft in the great newspaper center of New York, while Raynes spent his life on the banks of the Piscataqua. But when Raynes built a ship, especially his clippers, it was a poetic creation, with its tall masts and snow-white canvas. Such was the man's sense of line, symmetry and proportion that were he alive today he would probably be working for a giant aircraft company, designing the jet clippers of the sky.

The late Gertrude Pickett of New Castle, New Hampshire, whose husband descended from one of Raynes's ship-building rivals, frankly wrote that Raynes was by far the leading constructor of three-masted vessels, including clippers. She added:

> The Raynes Shipyard was in operation not only during Portsmouth's Heyday in Shipbuilding (1840-1860), but also for 12 years previously, a total of 32 years. No other local shipyard of this

*George Raynes, master clipper builder. Loaned by Kennard M. Palfrey, Jr., to Portsmouth Athenaeum.*

period equalled or surpassed this record. Within 32 years, the Raynes Shipyard turned out a total of 61 vessels, of which 50 were three-masted ships, two were barks, four were brigs, and five were schooners.[1]

George Raynes was born in 1799, in York, Maine, probably in the Raynes Neck vicinity. The date that he completed his formal schooling is not known, but before reaching manhood he made his way to the Maritime Provinces, there learning some of the basics of his trade.[2] By 1821 he was in Portsmouth, and was described in the first town directory as a boat builder living on South Street. It is most probable that he worked for Jacob Remick in the former Rindge Shipyard in the North End. Remick built several small vessels during the 1820s, including one, the *Emily*, a 323-ton brig, which flipped over on her beam ends when she hit the water on launching.[3] Although Remick was the builder, many years later, Raynes's name was associated in the public mind with that 1823 mishap.

Whatever the case, it is evident that by 1828 Raynes was running Remick's operation and had launched his first vessel, the *Planet*, a brig, rated at 129 tons. The *Planet* was followed by seven others from the stocks in that yard, the last being the *Harriet and Jesse*, a ship of 453 tons, and Raynes's largest ship up to that time. The *Harriet and Jesse* was launched September 12, 1832. But the Remick-Rindge yard was small, and George Raynes's ambitions were large. To realize them, on October 13, 1832, Raynes and William Neal, a shipmaster, bought what was known in Portsmouth as the Boyd Estate. They paid $3,815 for the property, the seller being Hannah Murray of New York, one of the last Boyd heirs. Because there has been much filling in over the years, it is next to impossible to define the original bounds, especially as one of the orientation points reads: "beginning at the corner post of the old fence standing on a jog seven feet from the Easterly side by the Bridge ..."[4] Two commercial buildings now stand in the general area—the stately Boyd Mansion having been torn down years ago to make way for a lumber yard. Raynes bought the mansion, as well as the shipyard he was to make famous. The whole property had been owned by Colonel George Boyd, one of Portsmouth's wealthiest merchants and shipbuilders in the years before the Revolutionary War. The house was built by Nathaniel Meserve, who had a shipyard in the rear of his home. "After his death in 1758, at the second siege of Louisburg, the house passed into the possession of Peter Livius. Col. George Boyd purchased the place about 1768, and considerably enlarged it ..."[5] Livius was a Loyalist, who left the country before Boyd's purchase. Meserve had built the *America*, a fourth-rate warship, there for the Royal Navy in 1749, but long before that royal favor the yard had been engaged in shipbuilding.

Boyd refitted the mansion and furnished it in the elegant style affordable only by the wealthy. A local descendant of Raynes was once told that the mansion had a long ballroom, finished with mahogany paneling and highlighted by huge mirrors. George Raynes's seeming desire to stay out of the public eye makes it doubtful that any balls were held there in his time, and the inventory of furnishings in Raynes's probate records confirms that he lived modestly indeed. The ballroom would have been more useful to Raynes as a mould loft, but it is doubtful that Eleanor Kennard Raynes would have allowed that in her house—not with six growing children.

The new shipyard ownership was described in the *Portsmouth Directory* for 1839 as Neal & Raynes. It is probable that Neal helped both with financing and practical advice on the building of ships. Once the property had been acquired, George Raynes wasted no time in laying the keel of a ship, the *Pontiff*. On April 13, 1833, *The Portsmouth Journal* reported:

> On Saturday last [April 6], the large and elegant ship *Pontiff* was launched from the shipyard of Neal & Raynes. *Pontiff*, in size, materials and workmanship, is in the first class of ships ever built in this place.

The *Pontiff* was not as lucky as many of Raynes's ships. She went to New Orleans from New York in May. Late in December, en route to Le Havre, she was wrecked on Rum Key in the Bahamas. First reports had both ship and cargo as a total loss, but later it was learned that 1,500 of the 1,820 bales had been saved by "wreckers," and taken into Nassau.

With the launch of the *Pontiff* from the former Boyd-Meserve yard, Raynes was off on a career that would see him launch fourteen more ships before 1840, and thirteen others in the 1840s before he began catering to the craze for clippers. His success enabled Raynes to buy out William Neal on March 17, 1838, at a cost of $10,000. Neal had done well out of his original investment, but Raynes was now in sole control of the shipyard.[6]

Only by inference or implication is it possible to get a feeling for George Raynes, the man. His marriage with Eleanor Kennard was apparently a happy one, and the union produced six children—Nathaniel K., George, Jr., William H., Ellen, Emma, and Ida. There is a hint that Ida may have been his favorite because he named a 303-ton brig the *Ida Raynes* in 1854, and still owned her at the time of his death. Ida Raynes married into the Palfrey family, and her descendants still reside in the Piscataqua Valley. Those who bought his ships heaped paeans on him, and it is wondered which of his clippers was his favorite. Yet even as the clipper mania increased, Raynes, in 1851, took time out to build and proudly launch twin schooners, the *Minna* and the *Brenda*, each with 300 tons displacement, for the coastal trade in the China Sea.

Although the *Roman* is deemed Raynes's first clipper, a description of a ship he launched just before her, late in 1849, shows he was already sensitive to the demand for sleeker, more luxurious vessels. The *North Atlantic* was intended for both passengers and freight, and her hailing port was New York. Despite the *North Atlantic*'s near qualifications, the *William E. Roman* was the first of the eight clippers built before George, Jr., became a partner.

Obviously, Raynes needed the skilled services of many artisans in the construction of his vessels. The names of some of these craftsmen have lived through the years. First and foremost was George, Jr., who was personally trained by his father. Another was Samuel L. Fernald, who died in Eliot at the age of seventy-three. His obituary reported that "in his younger days he was a skillful mechanic on the shipyard of the late George Raynes of this city, where his services were always required at his own option at every time of the commencement of the building of a new ship there. At the time of the falling off of the private shipbuilding on the river, Fernald was engaged in the mast and spar shop at the Navy Yard."[7] Many of the workmen around the clipper ships were specialists like Fernald. They went from yard to yard, performing their particular tasks. An outstanding example was David Junkins who came to the Piscataqua from York at the age of seventeen, and was apprenticed to his uncle, Isaac Junkins, then foreman of ship carpenters at the Portsmouth Navy Yard. When things quieted at the Navy Yard, after the War of 1812 ended, Junkins went to Durham to work for Joseph Coe, a master shipbuilder with a yard on the Oyster River. Junkins came to Portsmouth to work for George Raynes on the *Planet*, and after that worked for Thomas Cottle in Kittery, returning to Raynes's employment in 1830, beginning a long association with that yard until it closed. When that happened, Junkins worked in various yards, such as Tobey & Littlefield, Daniel Marcy's, and back on the Navy Yard. Such was the esteem in which he was held that all the Raynes apprentices were placed under his instruction. They called him "Uncle David." David Junkins sired thirteen children. At the time of his decease, at the age of eighty-five, eight were still living.[8]

Again, it must be emphasized that many of these skilled practitioners followed their trades at various yards, going to them when their specialties were needed. Another of these workmen was James Norton Wilson who died in 1894. Norton attended local schools, was apprenticed to the caulker's trade, and followed it "until 1888, when he suffered a

*Raynes family tombstone, Union cemetery, Portsmouth. Author's photograph.*

shock. He worked in all the shipyards on the river, and for many years on the Navy Yard."[9] George Lane came to America from England, made his home on Russell Street, and became a "whipsawyer," one of the best in Portsmouth at manipulating the long, narrow rip blade. He had lucrative employment in various shipyards. One of the most skilled of the finishing carpenters employed by Raynes, and other builders, was Frank Hunter, who died in 1895 at seventy-five. Many other of these craftsmen will be mentioned in the stories of the various clipper-building yards.

George Raynes, master builder, died April 12, 1855. His estate totaled nearly $90,000, and was placed in trust for his widow, Eleanor Kennard Raynes, and for his children. He stipulated that if Eleanor remarried she would forfeit her interest. Final division was to take place when all the Raynes children had died. Apparently only George, Jr., had enthusiasm for the shipyard, and he was given the right to buy out the vested interests of his siblings. Nathaniel K. Raynes went to Texas, where he was postmaster in Twin Sisters, Blanco County, in 1859. The Raynes shipyard did not last long after the death of the master. George, Jr. built the *Shooting Star*, the last of the Piscataqua clippers, in 1859, but then conveyed all his rights and interests to William H. Y. Hackett, as assignee, in order to meet the demands of his creditors. Hackett later advertised an assignee's sale "of valuable ship's timber, lumber and tools."[10] William F. Fernald bought the yard in 1863, and turned out several fine ships, among them the *Jean Ingelow* and the *Chocoura*.

Eleanor Kennard Raynes, the daughter of Nathaniel and Ruth (Walker) Kennard, died on January 20, 1895, after forty years of widowhood, in the home she had shared with her husband and children. She was born on the one-time School Street, September 8, 1809, and is buried beside her husband under the granite shaft in Union Cemetery.

## William E. Roman

SPECIFICATIONS: *Tonnage, 774. Length, 152.5 feet; breadth, 33.8; depth, 16.65. Owners, Joseph D. Taylor, Robert N. Oliphant and David C. Oliphant.*

THE ROMAN WAS GEORGE RAYNES'S first venture in the fast-developing craft of clipper building, and she was the first of the twenty-eight launched on the Piscataqua. Her name was really *William E. Roman,* possibly from a friend of the Oliphants, but in most listings she is simply the *Roman.* She was built to meet the demands of the fast-growing tea trade with its need for speedy vessels to run between China and Europe and the United States. Under Captain William Putnam, she entered that intense competition as soon as she was ready for sea. Raynes himself is supposed to have said that the *Roman* was "a medium clipper," being only 4.5 times as long as her breadth. Only one other Raynes clipper, the *Tinqua,* was smaller. But the *Roman* made creditable speed. On her only passage to San Francisco, the *Roman* made that port in 120 days, a better mark than those achieved by some of the other Raynes clippers. Of that passage, it was reported on May 28, 1853 from San Francisco that the *Red Rover* had landed her cargo in good order. "*Roman* landed hers in tolerable good order; *Danube* wet some packages."[11] It should be noted that all three of these square-riggers were Piscataqua-built, although the *Danube* was not a clipper.

On her return, under a Captain Hepburn, the *Roman* met her end. The first hint of a problem came from New York when the clipper *R. B. Forbes* arrived from Calcutta.[12] She reported that in latitude 27° 35' north, longitude 68° west, south and west of Bermuda, "fell in with ship *Roman,* Capt. Hepburn, 117 days from Canton, for New York, in sinking condition, having experienced very heavy weather and became unmanageable. *R. B. Forbes* took off Captain Hepburn, three officers and eight seamen. At 9 a.m. brig *William Price* came up, and took off seven remaining seamen and one passenger, and lay by her until we left her."[13] The *Roman* had on board a "valuable cargo of tea and silk consigned to Oliphant & Son." The *William Price* brought the eight she rescued into Philadelphia on December 21, 1853, with the added report the captain had fired the *Roman* before abandoning her. From Carl Cutler comes the remark:

> Among the full-built American tea ships perhaps the best work, all things considered, was that off *Roman,* still under Putnam. She left Woosung [China], on the 23rd of July [1851], exactly 13 days after the little British clipper *Reindeer* is reported

to have left, and arrived at London on Dec. 1, five days after the arrival of the *Reindeer*. For a ship of her type, her passage of 120 days against the monsoon must be considered good. It will be remembered that Woosung is nearly 850 miles farther up the coast than Canton. In the favorable monsoon season this usually involves four or five days sailing at the most, but with the monsoon ahead it may extend the passage for weeks.[14]

Sea Serpent, *passing South Head, San Francisco. Copy of a Chinese painting. Photograph by Mary Anne Stets. Mystic Seaport Museum collection.*

## Sea Serpent

SPECIFICATIONS: *Extreme. Tonnage, two listed, 1,337 and 1,402. Length, overall, 212; breadth, 39 feet; depth of hold, 21 feet. Owners, Grinnel & Minturn Co. of New York.*

THE *SEA SERPENT* was the largest vessel built on the Piscataqua River in the first half of the nineteenth century, and perhaps it was her size and subsequent fame that has caused some noted authorities to believe she was Raynes's first clipper. However, that honor went to the *William E. Roman*, as related above. Nevertheless, the *Sea Serpent* collected many laurels on her own. As her name implies, the *Sea Serpent*'s decor had a strong sea serpent motif, and rightly so. Almost daily, tales of serpents rising out of the sea were publicized along the East Coast. Two of the shiny, slivery, glistening creatures were entwined on the *Sea Serpent*'s stern. She was launched on November 20, 1850, and was described as being "sharp as a wedge, and it is believed by ship fanciers the wind will drive her through the water with great velocity."[15] *The Boston Atlas* said:

> THE CLIPPER SHIP SEA SERPENT — This is the second clipper on a large scale which has been built in New England this season; the *Surprise*, built at East Boston, was the first. The *Sea Serpent* is about 1300 tons.... She is very sharp forward and beautifully proportioned aft, without being cut up like a centerboard, and broadside on she looks rakish and saucy. To use a nautical phrase, "Her model fills the eye like a full moon....

The reporter for *The Boston Atlas*, a few days later, told how the *Sea Serpent* was built under the superintendence of Capt. William Howland, by George Raynes, who "is one of the most experienced mechanics in the country. His work is uniformly strong and well put together; and his models, when left to his own judgment, show his genius as a designer.... She is neatly rigged and looks very snug about the mastheads. Mr. Charles Harrat of Portsmouth rigged her, and it is but simple justice to state that his work will compare favorably alongside of that of the best New York riggers. Aloft, as well as below, she looks the saucy clipper, to the rope yarn." After the *Sea Serpent* arrived in New York, *The New York Herald* said:

> Her bow partakes of the wedge in appearance, and she is very sharp, but her lines are nearly all rounded. Her bow is tastefully ornamented with a large guilded eagle, with outstretched wings, beautifully carved, and has a simple and very neat appearance. Her hull is entirely black, excepting a narrow yellow

line which relieves the sameness and looks much smarter than the white streak so common on other vessels.

The model of the *Sea Serpent* is one that the greatest grumbler would be at a loss to find the smallest fault with. Head on she has most rakish appearance, and her lines swell along the bow into their utmost fullness, and then taper off again into the clean run. They show incontestably that the "line of beauty" has been made the guide in her construction. They are as perfect as perfection itself.[16]

The *Sea Serpent*'s first captain was William Howland, a martinet of an officer, then in his mid-forties. Captain Howland wore gloves at all times, and spoke only to the mates, who relayed his orders, almost man o' war style. The captain stayed in Portsmouth during the construction of the *Sea Serpent*, a vessel he came to love. She was the first ship to leave the Piscataqua at the end of a tow line. After the *Sea Serpent*, the famous tug, the *R. B. Forbes*, handled many of the tows from the Piscataqua shipyards.

The *Sea Serpent*'s owners decided to use her as a double-edged tool: not only would she be on the New York–San Francisco run, but from the West Coast she would go to China to load with tea. In four years she made four such voyages under Captain Howland. She left New York on her maiden voyage on January 11, 1851, with the goal of making the Golden Gate in less than a hundred days, but weather intervened, as it so often did when the clippers were making bids for records, which was nearly every time out. The *Sea Serpent* reached Valparaiso, Chile, in seventy-two days, where she put in for repairs that cost her eight days. Once cleared, another forty-five days were spent in running to San Francisco, which gave her a total time of 127 days, less the eight spent in repairs. From San Francisco she was forty-two days to Hong Kong, and, leaving Whampoa on October 16, 1851, she was 100 days to New York. Her second round-the-world voyage took only nine months and twenty-five days, including time spent in various ports.

From the very beginning there was nothing but praise after her voyages. Shortly after the first one, when George Raynes had already been paid a $1,500 bonus by the owners, one of them wrote to Raynes:

> We continue to be much pleased with the performance of *Sea Serpent* and in justice to you feel bound to say that we do not own a ship that has given us more satisfaction. She looks as well now as the day she was launched. There is not the slightest appearance of weakness or defect about her. Captain Howland speaks of her in the highest terms and we feel you have the right to be proud of her. We think we are safe in saying that there is not a clipper afloat that can rank higher than she.[17]

It would be easy to write thousands of words about the *Sea Serpent* because her story was one of continuing successful service. Captain J. D. Whitmore relieved Captain Howland in April, 1855, and in her first passage under him the *Sea Serpent* ran into a lot of trouble. She lost her maintopmast, split some sails and suffered other damage that necessitated putting in to Rio de Janeiro. After the repairs she took only eighty-one days to get from Rio to San Francisco, including time trying to get into port. In 1856, one of her crew, J. E. Davis, fell overboard and drowned on July 21, but that was not publicly known until she arrived in San Francisco in October. After unloading, the *Sea Serpent* was in a speed run to Honolulu, racing against six other clippers. The *Serpent's* time of fourteen days won the contest. Captain Whitmore, who had once commanded the Raynes-built *Tinqua*, died in December, 1860, while crossing the Indian Ocean on the home leg from Hong Kong. Williams, the mate, finished the voyage. The *Sea Serpent* was then taken over by Captain Samuel W. Pike, recently of the *Mameluke*. In turn, Pike was succeeded by Captain Thorndike, who had commanded the *Live Yankee*. Then there was a Captain Winsor in 1864, who was relieved by Captain Jeremiah D. White, who had her until she was sold.

Bayard Taylor, in 1853, wrote at length about the *Sea Serpent* while traveling from China to New York.[18] He kept almost a daily log of the journey, and closed his journal as she entered New York:

> We had a tedious night, of alternate calms and snow squalls, and I slept very little, out of anxiety lest a stiff nor'wester should spring up and blow us out to sea again. But by morning we had a pilot aboard, and taking advantage of a shift of the wind, made a tack which brought us in sight of Sandy Hook and of two steam tugs. At 10 o'clock the *Leviathan*, had grappled us; the useless sails were furled, and we sped surely and swiftly in the clear winter sunshine, up the outer bay, through the Narrows and into the noble harbor of New York. The hills of Staten Island glittered with snow; the trees long bare and the grass dead; and for the first time in nearly three years I looked upon a winter landscape. It was the 20th of December, 101 days since our departure from Whampoa. We rapidly approached the familiar and beloved city, and at 2 P.M. I landed on one of the East River piers.[19]

A young seaman on the *Sea Serpent*, Hugh McC. Gregory, kept a journal of the ship's fourth voyage around the world, beginning February 24, 1854. *The Sea Serpent Journal* is a published document, which clearly depicts the life of a foremast hand in clipper days. Young Gregory was on the larboard (port) watch under the first mate. He was a dropout from Trinity College, Hartford, Connecticut, and might have been added to the

*Serpent*'s crew because his father was a friend of Captain Howland. Certainly he enjoyed a little closer relationship to the commander than that accorded his fellows, being given the ship's position each day for use in his journal. Gregory's voyage began as Taylor's ended, and only the highlights of his observations are possible here. Saturday, March 25, 1854, he recorded:

> All morning I had to pass water to wash the pump well out with. And, oh God, how I suffered. Hardly able to crawl, I was made to carry and pump over 200 buckets of water. When I got done I was nearly crazy with pain. Perhaps I am too proud, but nevertheless I will go on with the ship's duties if I die for it, rather than ask leave to go on the sick list....
>
> Thursday, April 13—...For the last day or so I have been Jimmy Ducks, a title which I by no means relish. Jimmy Ducks is the title given to one who feeds the chickens and pigs. And a most unruly set of subjects are the pigs to feed, for when you come within sound of them such a squealing as is set up I never heard equalled by anything ashore.... The only emolument belonging to the office is the privilege of hooking fresh water enough to wash in, providing the mate doesn't catch you....
>
> Monday, April 24 — A most lovely morning, the sun shining bright and warm. The Horn, about 10 miles distant, and the adjacent isles formed a most striking picture. A solemn gray, such as one often reads about in the painted language of romance, cast its gloomy tints over the cliffs, which as day drew on gave way to shades of blue....
>
> Tuesday, April 25—Wind from the east all night, and at 1 a.m. passed the pitch of the Cape.... At daylight the land was nowhere to be seen, and all hands congratulated themselves that they were in the Pacific and around the Horn....
>
> Thursday, January 4—This morning I was subjected to one of a series of mean petty spite vented on me by Mr. Lind [a mate]—I suppose because he never has had his due amount of respect shown him and because I insulted him in Shanghai one afternoon by doubting his word, and had some high words with him about it— for he broke into my hen coop. He also killed one of Bob's fowl, a noble Shanghai, by his brutally knocking it around while it was in the coop.
>
> Friday, January 5—During the night someone tarred Lind's monkey, and great was the row that was raised. The mate said that as the tarring has begun he would give us a chance to finish it, so he got out the tar and set the Starboard watch, who did it, at work until he found the guilty one....
>
> Thursday, February 15—At daylight made sail, shook reefs out of the courses...and stood in. The pilot gave his opinion pretty

freely to the mate about matters being particularly severe on our being so shorthanded.... The Captain under the influence of liquor (intoxicated) all day and quarreling with the steward. Whatever happens to me, God deliver me from a drunken Captain. The men are all well nigh discouraged and curse him openly and loudly....

Friday, February 16 — Passed the "Narrows" and so ends my first voyage.

Hugh Gregory had been gone almost a year when he penned those final paragraphs and they probably explain why Captain Howland was relieved after that fourth voyage. The comparison between the closing paragraphs of Taylor's journal and those written by Gregory is striking: one was written by a passenger, the other by a worker.

The *Sea Serpent* continued her profitable voyaging under the ownership of Grinnel, Minturn & Company until May, 1874, when she was sold to a Norwegian merchant who quickly sold her to a firm in his homeland. In 1883, renamed *Progress*, she was again sold. On June 12, 1891, bound from Quebec for Dublin with a cargo of lumber, she was abandoned at sea to the ignominious fate of being a derelict, a drifting hulk, that posed a threat to other ships. Before she finally disappeared, she was known to have drifted 1,120 miles in ninety-three days, and was reported nineteen times by other vessels.

Gone, but not forgotten! In 1939, as the United States was rebuilding its merchant fleet, one of the new freighters was named the *Sea Serpent* in honor of the doughty clipper.[20] The twentieth century *Sea Serpent* was a C2, cargo-type vessel, built in Chester, Pennsylvania, by Sun Shipbuilding. She served in World War II, and was scrapped in Savona, Italy, on August 24, 1971.

## Wild Pigeon

*SPECIFICATIONS: Tonnage, 996. Length, 178 feet, 189 feet over all; breadth, 35 feet; depth, 20 feet. Owners, the Oliphants of New York.*

THE WILD PIGEON may well have been the fastest vessel George Raynes sent down the building ways. Five hundred tons smaller than the *Sea Serpent*, she was his third clipper. Launched on July 31, 1851, the *Wild Pigeon* left the Piscataqua under her own sail, headed for New York. She made the run in less than forty hours, with a Captain Buckingham in command.[21] She must have been a proud sight while lying at her berth in New York. A beautifully carved pigeon, depicted in flight, was her figurehead, and two gilded pigeons graced her stern. Everything about the *Wild Pigeon* testified to the skills of her builder. One writer said:

> The style of her construction is not surpassed for strength and workmanship by any vessel her size afloat. Her keel is of rock maple.... The between decks are of hard pine, 2½ inches thick, and the upper deck of white pine, of the same substance.... Her frame is entirely of white oak, the growth of New Hampshire.... She is seasoned with salt.... She is a full-rigged ship....[22]

Not only was the *Wild Pigeon* admired by waterfront habituees, but businessmen, with an eye to the fast movement of goods to the lucrative San Francisco market, were quick to seek her services. Under Captain George W. Putnam, the *Wild Pigeon* sailed from New York, on October 11, 1851, arriving in San Francisco on January 28, 1852, a span of 109 days. "Capt. Putnam reported his passage as 107 days in light winds. She was under three skysails for 75 days and for 24 consecutive days in the Pacific had skysails and royal studding sails set, and never shifted a rope."[23] Captain Putnam's claim was modest in comparison to what was reported in *The Boston Atlas,* March 3, 1852:

> The new clipper ship *Wild Pigeon*, Capt. Putnam, which sailed from New York, Oct. 14 made the shortest passage to San Francisco (102 days) of any vessel which sailed in October, having beaten the *Comet, Trade Wind* and *Golden Gate*, all magnificent New York clippers, the least of which is 500 tons larger than her. She sailed in company with *Golden Gate*, and ten to one were staked in New York in favor of the latter, yet *Wild Pigeon* never had wind enough during her passage to obtain her highest rate of speed.... Off Cape Horn she encountered a heavy gale, but

Wild Pigeon, *one of Raynes' fastest vessels. Portsmouth Athenaeum collection.*

*Captain Hanson commanded* Wild Pigeon *on a voyage from New York to San Francisco. The Mariners Museum collection.*

carried sail and was not hove to during passage.... Capt. Putnam writes that under every circumstance she proved to be a perfect vessel, so much so that he could not suggest an improvement in her....

Cutler put his faith in the ship's logs, and wrote, "The log of *Wild Pigeon* shows that she sailed as stated...and was anchored in the harbor of San Francisco on the 28th of January. This would make her elapsed time 106 days...[24] Her cargo on that passage included a bale of copper, 200 boxes of soap, eight pairs of iron doors, 108 tons of coal, 250 barrels of flour, three barrels of butter, thirty-nine wheel barrows, four kegs of shot, one piano, six cases of copper, 100 kegs of nails, ten dozen shovels, and miscellaneous merchandise, plus passengers.

Clippers were constantly in figurehead-to-figurehead competition. In addition to the commercial advantages of being in port ahead of others, there was the natural desire to best a rival. The *Wild Pigeon* was in such a contest in 1854, vying against the *Sweepstakes*, built by the Westervelts of New York, and the *Flying Fish* from Donald McKay's yard:

These three ships passed the Straits of Sunda, the *Sweepstakes* and *Wild Pigeon* in company and the *Flying Fish* four days previous; after repeatedly falling in with each other on passage, they arrived within 14 hours of the same time. The *Wild Pigeon* being the first reported, the *Sweepstakes*, then shortly after, the *Flying Fish*.[25]

In 1858, under the command of Captain P. N. Mayhew, the *Wild Pigeon* made the passage from Pisagua, Peru, to New York in fifty-one days. Two years later, with Mayhew still in command, she set a record for a passage from Talcahuano, Chile, to New York with a run of fifty days.[26] But none of these feats surprised those who knew her, and almost from the first, she was considered a lucky ship. An omen of great significance had been seen by superstitious seamen in the fact that on her run from Portsmouth to New York, right after launching, wild pigeons had alighted on the *Wild Pigeon*. The pigeons flew around the ship three times, and then one landed on the royal yard and another on the jib boom—indeed a portent of good fortune.

As the years went by, the *Wild Pigeon* continued to show her tail feathers to a lot of fast sailers. She went under the Union Jack in February, 1863, to keep her safe from the marauding Confederate cruisers. "And without change of name and still commanded by Captain Mayhew, she went from New York to Shanghai, later crossing from Hong Kong to San Francisco in 47 days. Thence to New York, via Valparaiso and back to the latter port, arriving April 7, 1865, in 80 days from New York. There she was reported sold for $35,000...."[27] The *Wild Pigeon* was bought by Spanish interests, becoming the *Bella Juana* in the registers of 1868.

Shortly after her sale, the *Wild Pigeon* played a role in one of the upheavals that occasionally plagued the Peruvian government at this period. Spain wanted to wrest control away from the Peruvians, and tried to impose its presence in the Chincha Islands with their rich guano beds. It was demanded that the American vessels loading there pay tribute for their cargoes. One of these ships was the *Sierra Nevada*, whose captain ignored the demand, and sailed for home. "The *Amazonas* followed in pursuit, but did not overhaul her."[28] It was also reported that the *Wild Pigeon* had been assigned the duty of transporting the Peruvian leader, Ramon Castillo, to some port in Europe, the purpose for which she had been bought a few months previously.[29] General Castillo died quietly in Peru, however, in 1868. The *Wild Pigeon* suffered another name change to *Voladora*, and was rerigged as a bark. On February 17, 1892, the former *Wild Pigeon* was abandoned in sinking condition, latitude 27° north, longitude 68° west, in the same general area where the *William E. Roman* had gone down forty years earlier.

Witch of the Wave, one of the most beautifully finished clippers. Painting attributed to Clement Drew. Peabody Museum of Salem collection.

## Witch of the Wave

> SPECIFICATIONS: *Extreme. Tonnage, 1,498. Length, at keel, 191 feet; over all, 220 feet; breadth, 40 feet; depth, 21 feet; seven feet between decks. Owners, Glidden & Williams, Twombley & Lamson of Boston and Captain John Bartram.*

**F**OR A SHORT TIME the *Witch of the Wave* enjoyed the distinction of being the most beautifully finished vessel ever launched on the Piscataqua, but the *Nightingale*, when she came down the ways a few weeks after her, immediately captured all honors for lavishness of finish. Beautifully appointed though they were, in the first year or two of their construction, the clippers were viewed with some abhorrence by the more conservative mariners who wryly commented that they were "beautiful vessels to look at, but too sharp to pay." The popularity of the clippers reached a climax in 1856-1857, then began to wane, while the old, standard packet-type ship continued in production. The clippers scored for a while because "the profitable freights obtained by many of these sharp vessels" dissipated the idea they were too sharp, "and now a new clipper is not universally regarded as a costly experiment.... The splendid appearance of *Witch of the Wave* has made us forget our prejudices." *The Boston Atlas* writer was right when he admitted the clippers were costly—the *Witch* was worth $90,000 when she slid into the water with her lower masts in place. The launching ceremony on April 5, 1851, offered the usual colorful scene, and because it was Saturday, more people were free to see it. It gave occasion, as usual, for some of the hyperbole that so delighted people 130 years ago. Hundreds of notables were on hand, and the more important of them were invited by the owners and the builder to have lunch on board. In the course of it, Ephraim Miller, collector of the port of Salem, Massachusetts, where the *Witch* was to be homeported, proposed a toast:

> Success to the newest and youngest of the Salem witches. Had they possessed a proportional share of her beauty, we are confident that the sternest tribunal before which any of them were arraigned, would never have the heart to subject a single one to the trial to which the successor is designed—Trial by Water.

Enthusiastic guests and spectators flocked to Portsmouth on May 2 to watch the *Witch of the Wave* leave the place of her creation. *The Salem Register* went all out in its report:

> ...The first morning train to Portsmouth was freighted with a large number of ladies and gentlemen from Boston, Salem and Newburyport, who, with the Portsmouth guests, made up a

company of two or three hundred persons. At 10½ o'clock A.M. the gallant ship, with all her bunting displayed, was cast loose from her fasts, and, grappled by the steamer, proceeded down the river, cheered to the echo by the multitudes who thronged the wharves, and by the sturdy ship-builders who gathered on the taff rail of another leviathan on the stocks in an adjacent shipyard. The compliment was returned, the band on board played "Hail Columbia" and the *Witch of the Wave* sped on her way.

Charles W. Brewster, editor of *The Portsmouth Journal*, published his regrets that other engagements prevented "our accepting a polite invitation to take a berth on her first trip; a large number of our citizens availed themselves of the *bewitching* opportunity."

Those lucky Portsmouth people who were on board were given the treat of seeing what a really fast clipper could do under sail. The *Witch*'s colors were streaming in the wind, as the Boston Cadet Band played "The Star-Spangled Banner." Once clear of Fort Constitution, and beyond Whale's Back, the tug, *R. B. Forbes*, moved away from the vessel's side and put tension on the tow line. It was the moment a proud George Raynes had been waiting for. With a keen sense of showmanship, and utter faith in his own handiwork, George Raynes suggested that Captain Bartram set a little sail, "just to assist the tow-boat a little."[30] The order was given, and Charles Harrat's crew of riggers swarmed aloft and loosened the topsails, jib and foretopmast staysail. The *Witch of the Wave* quickly ran up on the weather side of the tug, and was logged at 9½ knots. It was not only a proud moment for Raynes, but for craftsmen like William Martin and William D. Fernald who had constructed the spars, and for Charles Walker, the sailmaker. John Wilson won compliments for the skill of the cabin joiner work. Charles Harat no doubt was quite pleased with the chance to show off the skills of his riggers. It can be conjectured that, at that moment, the *Witch of the Wave* was her builder's favorite vessel.

Raynes's little bit of theatrics merely whetted the appetites of the Salem people on board for more tributes. *The Register* further reported:

> The time was passed most delightfully by those who escaped seasickness. A band of five or six pieces of music called the dancers to their feet, and others amused themselves in a variety of ways — the "old salts" turning their scrutiny to the performance of the ship, which excited their undisguised admiration. After rounding Thatcher's Island, a most bountiful dinner was spread on a table between decks, which accommodated the entire multitude.
> ...Mr. Derby made some excellent remarks in relation to commerce; navigation; the improvements in shipbuilding; the

Witch of the Wave, *a drawing by F. Della Motte.*
*National Maritime Museum, Greenwich, England.*

magnificent vessel on board which they were; her name, of course, directing his thoughts to some pleasant mention of the Salem witches....

These remarks were greeted with enthusiastic applause. The company were then favored with a song and chorus, which were received with apparant great satisfaction....

What came next was entitled "The Portsmouth Lament." One verse will suffice to give the general theme:

I wonder what's the dreadful row
    They're kicking up in Portsmouth now;

> The people running up and down,
> > Crying—"All Salem's come to town!
> > > Clear the way, the ship is starting!
> > > Clear the track, the ship is starting!
> > > Clear the track, the ship is starting!
> > > And Portsmouth hearts are sad at parting.

The "Lament" continued in that vein for eight more verses. Nor was Portsmouth backward at this lacrimose moment. *The Portsmouth Journal* reported that as the *Witch of the Wave* was leaving the Piscataqua forever and "an original and appropriate song was sung on board," in which were the following expressive lines:

> And the good ship flies, and the wind blows free
> As she leaps to her lover's arms—the Sea!

*The Salem Register* reported in its May 10 issue what was really an accolade to the *Witch of the Wave*:

> Salem, we are happy to know, is to have the honor of claiming among her commercial marine this magnificent specimen of naval architecture, the perfection of modern ship-building. She made a short visit to this port on Friday to obtain her Register, remained at anchor over night, and left for Boston on Saturday forenoon, in tow of the steamer *R. B. Forbes*.... She was launched on the 5th of April last, and will cost, fitted for sea, upwards of $90,000....
>
> The beautiful proportions and exquisite model of this vessel are unsurpassed, and invite the unqualified admiration of the experienced eye.
>
> Her cabin and staterooms are finished and furnished in the most superb style. The carpet, furniture and ornamental work are luxurious. The paneling is of birdseye maple, banded with satin wood; the pilasters of rosewood, banded with zebra wood; the whole exquisitely polished; the cornices and moulding, on the pure white ground, gilded. The medical department is accommodated with a permanent locker, an apothecary's shop, and fitted in a style corresponding with the cabin fixtures, perfectly neat and elegant. We noticed that the medicines were prepared and arranged with so much taste and skill by William R. Preston of Portsmouth, formerly of Salem....[31]
>
> The carved work on head and stern is most delicately and elaborately executed by Mr. John W. Mason of Boston. The figure head represents a beautiful female, in gossamer drapery, shielded by a broad shell like a canopy, gracefully and lightly stepping on the crest of a wave, emblematic of the ship's name.

Witch of the Wave *in Boston Harbor before her maiden voyage. From Gleason's Magazine.*

When the *Witch of the Wave* arrived in Boston, new praises were directed to her. Much of what was said had already been reported both in Salem and Portsmouth, but the reporter for *The Boston Atlas* added some information not previously printed:

> ...She has no apparent transom outside, but the stern is at once formed on the rudder case, with a slight rake aft as it rises. Upon it is a representation of her name, floating in a shell with an imp, on the larboard [port] side riding a dolphin, and on the other side other members of the finny family sporting in the sea. Above these is her name in gilded letters, and below it her port of hail.... Her name in gilded letters is also placed on her bulwarks, between the main and mizzen rigging....
>
> She has three cabins, the first contains the captain's stateroom on the starboard side, which overlooks that side of the main deck, and near it is a stateroom for the steward. Abaft these, on the same side is the pantry. On the opposite side are staterooms for the officers and a water closet.
>
> This cabin is wainscotted and grained, and forms an ante-room to that abaft it, which is the great cabin. Here is

splendor! . . . The transom is fitted as a semi-circular sofa, covered with rich velvet. Her after cabins contain seven large staterooms and two water closets, and their furniture, together with that of the staterooms, is truly magnificent. . . . She also has a library of over 100 volumes.

From the eloquence of the descriptive passages, it becomes obvious that while a journey to San Francisco or other world ports might take months, the traveler did not suffer for want of luxurious surroundings; "cabin fever," as modern idiom has it, might be a problem, but not comfort. The impression comes through most strongly that George Raynes put his soul into his creations. But the *Witch of the Wave* was not intended to be an *objet d'art*; she had serious work to do. Towed into Boston on May 3, she was loaded for San Francisco in seventeen days, sailing on May 20. Her passage to San Francisco was 123 days, which was not particularly good time; she bettered it by six days on a later trip. From California, she was forty days to Hong Kong, thence to Canton, where she loaded with 19,000 chests of tea for London. That passage took ninety-one days, a record performance up to that time. *The Illustrated London News* was ecstatic over *Witch of the Wave*, saying, "She is the object of much interest as she lies at the dock. Her bows are similar to those of a large cutter yacht." Other plaudits came her way. One of her officers wrote that parties in London had offered to buy her:

> They would like to take the ship up, or even purchase her, to run between Bombay and China. They are all delighted with her. Mr. [Richard] Green, celebrated shipowner of London [Who was also a noted shipbuilder.], has examined her thoroughly, and tells me that Englishmen must go to school again before they can compete with the Americans. I think we have had half of London on board to look at her.
> She is regarded by all who have seen her, at home and abroad, a new specimen of naval architecture. . . .[32]

The *Witch of the Wave* was in India Dock on the River Thames, and it was reported that her fast time from Canton was a subject of eulogy in *The London Times* on April 16. "She has made one of the quickest passages from China to London ever recorded, 85 days to Land's End, and notwithstanding she had to beat all the way up the English Channel for eight days, she was only 92 days from port to port." The *London Shipping Gazette* said she "worked to the windward of 400 sailing vessels bound up the channel, and not a single vessel on the passage could keep way with her." While *The Portsmouth Journal* was quite proud in reporting the above in its May 1, 1852, issue, but the editor was more than a little annoyed that the London accounts described the *Witch of the Wave* as a New York-built clipper. Brewster snorted:

> Englishmen are too apt to regard New York as being the United States, and everything belonging to this country as New York property. — But the *Witch of the Wave* is a child of the Piscataqua River, built by George Raynes, Esq....

From London it was back to Boston, and a change of command. Captain Benjamin Tay relieved Captain J. H. Millet for her second globe-girdling voyage. Captain Tay claimed 116 days to San Francisco, but it was actually 119. A correspondent of *The Boston Traveller* wrote that "*Witch of the Wave* arrived in less time than her maiden voyage. She discharged her goods in as good condition as when taken aboard. She's a great favorite of the San Francisco merchants." And she was also a great favorite with her passengers on that run. They presented Captain Tay with a silver pitcher and a resolution:

> Resolved, that although our expectations were much raised in the far-famed ship *Witch of the Wave*, we have not been disappointed in one particular, as she has not only proved herself a fast sailer, passing every ship seen on the voyage, but her qualities as a sea boat are all that can be desired.[33]

Captain Lewis F. Miller commanded her on her third trip around the world, and he made the best time with her to San Francisco, 117 days, and beat out five top-notch clippers in doing it. When Miller brought her back to Boston, Captain Samuel V. Shreve took over. The *Witch* was loaded for Batavia in the Dutch East Indies; there she took on cargo for Amsterdam. After arrival in Holland, she returned to Batavia, and then back to Holland, where she was sold to a Dutch firm. What she did under various foreign flags is not known, but while still flying the stars and stripes she set a Calcutta–Boston record — eighty-one days — that has never been equalled or beaten, though she beat the clipper *Staffordshire* by only one day. Renamed *Electra*, the *Witch* continued in Dutch service until 1882, when she was sold to a Norwegian firm and given the name *Ruth*.

## Tinqua

SPECIFICATIONS: *Tonnage, 668. Length, 145 feet; breadth, 31.9 feet; depth, 19 feet. Owners, Oliphant & Co., New York.*

THE SMALLEST OF THE CLIPPERS George Raynes sent to sea, the *Tinqua*, followed the *Wild Pigeon* and the *Witch of the Wave*, being launched on October 2, 1852. She was intended for the China trade. Marine architects saw more of a resemblance to the *Wild Pigeon* than to the *Witch*, and her size indicated that the Oliphants wanted much the same style, but in a vessel two-thirds the size of the *Wild Pigeon*.

If the *Tinqua* had been able to make more passages to the West Coast, she might have established herself as one of the speediest in the business for her size. Captain Jacob D. Whitmore, a famed driver of clippers, superintended her construction from the laying of the keel by the skillful Samuel L. Fernald to the final touches of paint. The owners named her *Tinqua* in honor of one of the leading merchants in Canton, China, with whom they were associated. The *Tinqua* left the Piscataqua twenty-four days after launching, under tow by the tug *Achilles*, going directly to New York for loading. Arriving there on October 27, she quickly took on cargo for a round-the-world voyage, via San Francisco. The *Tinqua* cleared New York on November 24. *The Chronicle* reported on April 1 that the *Tinqua* had been spoken January 19 off Cape Horn where she had been for seven days, but she arrived in San Francisco on March 19, in the fairly good time of 115 days. Of Raynes's clippers only the *Sea Serpent* and the *Wild Pigeon* registered faster runs to the west coast; moreover, in her two trips, the *Tinqua* averaged 119 days, compared to 123½ days for six passages by the *Sea Serpent*, and 123 in four for the *Wild Pigeon*.

The *Tinqua* quickly discharged her cargo on that first run, and sailed for Hong Kong, arriving in Honolulu fifteen days later, and she was at Manila on June 16. Early in August, she was loading in Canton for New York.[34] She was back in New York by December 10, after passing through a heavy gale on November 26, in which she lost her jib boom, top gallantmast, and a whole suit of sails. She also lost all her fresh water, but was resupplied on December 3 by Captain Conway of the ship *Prince de Joinville*.

For her next voyage, the *Tinqua* went to Philadelphia to load, from which port she was towed to sea on Februray 11, 1854, headed for San Francisco. In July she was at Shanghai, loaded, and headed back to New

*Tinqua, off Hong Kong, a Chinese port painting.*

York in October. She almost made it. In its January 30, 1855, issue *The Chronicle* reported:

> How Ships Are Lost—*The Boston Traveller* says of the ship *Tinqua*, which struck on the outer shoal of Cape Hatteras, "when the crew left her, she was full of water, but with her masts still standing, and when last seen was drifting northeast, and if fallen in with would be found in the Gulf Stream. The stern was all under water. The captain had not sounded before she struck, supposing himself 40 miles east of where he was.
>
> Schooner *R. L. Myers*, at New York on the 17th from Washington, N.C., had on board master and part of the crew of the *Tinqua*, Shanghai for New York, the *Tinqua* having gone on shore on Friday last [Jan. 12] in a thick fog and went to pieces. Commanded by Capt. Jacob Whitmore, and owned by Oliphant & Son, she measured 700 tons. The vessel with a cargo of teas and silks was a total loss. Crew saved and picked up by three different vessels. The vessel and freight valued at $60,000, the cargo at $290,000.

Cutler quotes from a New York newspaper that the *Tinqua* on her first passage, "under the veteran driver, Jacob D. Whitmore," made one of the best runs of the year, after facing a roaring nor'wester going around the Horn:

> He had run to within 200 miles of the Line [Equator] in 13 days. One can only imagine the way the "Old Man" carried sail to accomplish this unprecedented feat. The *Tinqua* was a new ship very heavily rigged with the best Russian hemp by men who were masters of their art. Yet Whitmore drove her so hard that his rigging slacked off [stretched], not once but several times, and each time he was compelled to heave to and set it up—a fact which must have cost many hours delay in the aggregate. It is no hasty job to set up a ship's rigging, even under ordinary conditions of doldrum weather, where such work is usually done. Reading between the lines it is altogether probable that *Tinqua* was delayed a fully 24 hours in this manner....[35]

They were hard-bitten men, those captains who drove the clippers around the Horn to San Francisco, and then on to circle the globe. They had to be. Speed was the essence of the business: the sooner they arrived with a cargo in good condition—at New York, Boston or London—the better the price.

## Wild Duck

*SPECIFICATIONS: Tonnage, 860. Length, 175 feet; breadth, 33.6 feet; depth, 29 feet; Owners, Oliphant & Co.*

THE LAUNCHING OF THE *WILD DUCK* marked an occasion of sorts for George Raynes. She was the fiftieth vessel he had built since the *Planet* in 1828, when he first became a master shipbuilder, and she was the fourth clipper he had fabricated for the Oliphants, a strong testimony to their satisfaction with his creations. The *Wild Duck* was bigger than the *Tinqua* by nearly 200 tons. Experts thought she resembled the *Wild Pigeon*, although the latter was a hundred tons heavier. Because the scope of this work is limited to square-rigged vessels, classified as clippers, the impression might be that Raynes, had succumbed to the clipper mania that pervaded shipping circles, but that is far from the truth. For example, after he launched the *Sea Serpent* in 1850, he built the *George Raynes* (999 tons), and the *Constantine* (1,161 tons) in that same year. The *Orient*, at 1,561 tons, followed the *Witch of the Wave* and the *Wild Pigeon* in 1851. They were followed by the *Tinqua* and the *Wild Duck*.

Despite the name given her, the *Wild Duck*'s figurehead was an eagle on the wing "while on her handsome round stern there was a sporting dog, surrounded by gilt scroll work." Perhaps the dog was supposed to represent a retriever in the shooting of wild ducks. A news item of November 26, 1852, said that Raynes was under contract with the Oliphants for a California and Canton clipper, to be called the *Stranger*.[36] It could be that the intended name was what occasioned the eagle figurehead. On April 12, 1853, the *Wild Duck*, as she was then being called, was launched. After the ceremony, *The Chronicle* reported:

> The beautiful ship *Wild Duck*...is lying at wharf of Mr. Raynes, the builder. She is worth an examination of everyone who can appreciate the union of beauty and strength. She will ride over the billows as gaily as the water fowl whose name she bears — which, by the way, would be a capital model for the craft, combining the propelling and sailing qualities. Mr. Raynes has a very busy scene at his yard; one ship rigging, and another all framed and ready for planking.

Captain A. G. Hamilton took the *Wild Duck* down river on May 13, with the help of a harbor steamer—possibly the *Grace Darling*. The *Wild Duck* went to New York under her own sail, which was not customary. A few days later *The Chronicle* published a letter from a passenger on the New York run:

*Wild Duck,* an oil painting by J. E. Buttersworth.

> We left Pray's Wharf at 4:30 Friday afternoon with a fair wind which towards evening worked round to westward, and continued from that quarter till Thursday when we reached New York.
> The *Wild Duck* in this trip proved herself a fast sailer, as she passed everything we came in sight of, although, on account of being light [Not loaded] she could not sail as close to the wind as most of the vessels she overtook. As the log was not thrown during the voyage, the number of knots she sailed is not known. Her commander, Captain Hamilton, expressed himself perfectly satisfied with her; she works easy, is a fine sea boat, and adds one more to the long list of first-class ships built by George Raynes, Esq.
> She carried little sail during a 24-hour blow, and made no distance. Rolling caused seasickness among the passengers. *Wild Duck* outsailed a pilot boat that met her off the South Shoal, 200 miles from New York, and the pilot could not come on board until she reefed canvas. Heaved to Wednesday because of fog and got under way again Thursday morning. At 7 o'clock dropped anchor. At 1 p.m. a breeze sprang up, southeast, and she weighed anchor and hauled into the dock at the foot of Wall Street at 3 p.m.

Despite the glowing account of her speed to New York, the *Wild Duck* set no records in her three passages to San Francisco. In fact, of Raynes's clippers, she had the fourth slowest average—130 days. It must be noted, however, how much depended on the time of year when a vessel was inbound or outbound. The *Wild Duck* sailed from New York on July 2, 1853, taking 132 days to reach San Francisco. Difficult weather conditions kept the *Wild Duck* off Cape Horn for twelve days while she tried to get into the Pacific. Throughout that run she had nothing but light winds, having her skysails set throughout the final forty days to San Francisco. Her time to Shanghai was slow, seventy-two days, and she was 105 days back to New York. But even so, she managed to get top freight rates at Woosung, China: $20 a ton for tea and $30 for silks. With freight rates like that, it was no wonder American shipping firms were investing heavily in the fast-moving clippers. On her second voyage she showed but little more speed than on the previous journey, and Captain Hamilton turned her over to a Captain Ellery, who commanded her on her third voyage.[37] She fared little better on the New York–San Francisco leg, leaving the latter port on March 22, 1856, for Hong Kong, and going 300 more miles to Foo Chow Foo, where she loaded for New York. As she dropped down the River Min, she went ashore on Nokenga Bank. One account has it that the vessel and cargo ($270,000) were a total loss, but the crew was saved. Later it was reported that she had been floated and towed to Foo Chow Foo, but she does not appear in any more shipping records.

## Coeur de Lion

*SPECIFICATIONS: Tonnage, 1,098. Length, 182 feet; breadth, 36 feet; depth, 22 feet. Dead rise, 15 inches. Owners, William F. Parrott of Boston, and Capt. George W. Tucker of Portsmouth.*

**W**HY GEORGE RAYNES, or the owners, paid tribute to a long-dead English king in naming the *Coeur de Lion* is not known. No matter what the reason, the fact is that an effigy of Richard the Lionhearted graced the *Coeur de Lion*'s bow, while his coat of arms adorned the stern. As was true of all Raynes's vessels, the *Coeur de Lion*'s ornamental work was well executed.

She was launched on January 3, 1854, on a day in which the weather was so bad that it discouraged the large crowd that customarily attended Piscataqua launchings. Following ancient and honorable tradition, the ship's captain, George W. Tucker, paid tribute to the artisans who built her by entertaining them at dinner in the City Hotel on Congress Street.[38] Two weeks later, Captain Tucker took the *Coeur de Lion* down river, under tow by the *R. B. Forbes*, heading for Boston, to be loaded for San Francisco. *The Boston Argus* described her:

> ...Her stern is nearly semi-circular in outline, has little projection beyond the sternpost, and is very snug and neat. The mouldings of her main rail and planksheer are parallel, fore and aft, and will probably be gilded, if the weather will permit.... She is sheathed with yellow metal [A brass consisting of 60 parts copper and 40 parts zinc.]....
>
> The quarters for the crew are under the topgallant forecastle, and are a few feet below the upper deck. They are spacious, well arranged, and neatly fitted up.... She has a half poop deck with a small house in front, which contains the pantry and staterooms for the officers, and abaft this is a passage across, which leads to the cabins. Her after cabin is tastefully wainscotted with mahogany, relieved with enameled pilasters and cornices, edged with gilded mouldings and flowers. An oval mirror over the transom gives a reflected view of the cabin and there is a fine sofa aft, corresponding in outline with the curve of the stern. The furniture is costly and neatly arranged....
>
> Both cabins have spacious staterooms and other apartments on each side, and the accommodations are all that could be desired for safety and comfort...
>
> Her frame, wales, hooks, pointers and most of her knees are of New Hampshire white oak, and her ceiling of hard pine...and the decks are of white pine, 3½ inches thick, copper fastened fore and aft....

*Coeur de Lion, a painting by Chinese artist Chonc Qua. The Smithsonian Institution collection.*

Duncan McLean, *The Argus* reporter, lavished praise on the rigging of the *Coeur de Lion* as she lay at the Lewis Wharf in Boston, adding she "looks quite snug aloft, and even light compared with other clippers. To our eyes she is reasonably sparred, and we think will carry her canvas well and sail swiftly. Two paintings of the *Coeur de Lion* are in existence. One is by the famed Chinese artist, Chonc Qua, showing her in Hong Kong Harbor in 1855, and the other is modern, done by marine artist Francis A. Less'Ard, who worked from a photograph of the Chonc Qua painting. In writing of the *Coeur de Lion*, Less'Ard gets almost maudlin about the glamorous days of sailing ships:

> A century has passed, the half hull models lay in a cloud of dust, the old shipyards are now part of great brick and stone cities. The once clear harbor water is now stained with the pollution of modern man, oil blackened, as is the once beautiful shoreline where children played, romped, and perhaps dreamed of going to sea in tall sailing ships.

But to get back to the story of the *Coeur de Lion*, a vessel so well built that she lasted just over sixty-one years, an age surpassed among Piscataqua clippers only by the *Dashing Wave*. Captain Tucker took the *Coeur de Lion* out of Boston on February 5, 1854, for her first passage to San Francisco. She arrived on June 18, after a light-weather passage of 133 days. Her run to the Horn had taken sixty-four days, and she was seven days trying to get into the Pacific. From the West Coast, she went to Hong Kong, thence to Shanghai, nearly a thousand miles to the north, returning to New York on January 30, 1855. April 4, she again sailed to San Francisco, arriving on August 2, one of the seven clippers to glide through the Golden Gate in a single day, an event that was never repeated. Six months later she was back in New York, and sailed again for San Francisco on April 18, making what was her last Cape Horn passage. *The Chronicle* reported on October 1:

> The clipper ship *Coeur de Lion*, now lying at the Lombard Dock, in San Francisco (Says the *Alta Californian*) is one of the finest modeled and finished ships which we have ever seen in this port. In every place she has visited, her fine line, neat finish, finely proportioned spars, &c., have attracted universal attention and been the theme of praise by seafaring men, both American and foreign. She is the last ship built by George Raynes of Portsmouth, and considered the best of the splendid fleet constructed by him.... The *Coeur de Lion* is a medium-sized ship, carrying about 2,000 tons of cargo. She has thus far made three voyages from the Atlantic States to this city, turning out her cargo each time in

excellent order. She belongs to William F. Parrott of Boston, is commanded by Capt. George W. Tucker, and comes consigned to Bingham & Reynolds. In a few days, Captain Tucker will take departure for Hong Kong, carrying with him a number of the Flowery Kingdom [Chinese].

While at Hong Kong on that trip, the *Coeur de Lion* took on an unusual cargo—British troops destined for Calcutta, where she arrived, December 8, 1856, in the exceptionally fast time of twenty-six days. From Calcutta she went to Rangoon, and loaded there for England. After leaving Rangoon, she met the Dutch bark, the *Henrietta Maria*, which was flying distress signals. On boarding her, Captain Tucker learned she had been bound for Havana with Chinese coolies as cargo. Facing virtual slavery, the coolies rebelled, took possession of the vessel, and seized all the weapons. After that, the *Henrietta Maria*'s captain and part of the crew escaped in a boat while the cook jumped overboard and disappeared. Most of the coolies fled to the shore. Tucker put Chief Officer Crawford in command, with four members of his own crew, and they worked her back to Singapore, presumably for a good salvage fee.[39]

The *Coeur de Lion* then continued on her passage to Falmouth, England, but her career under the American flag was nearing an end. What happened, in part, was that the demand for clippers was beginning to decline. By 1857, when she was reported disengaged in Shanghai, there were many of them, all competing for cargoes in the same markets. That is why some of the proud clippers wound up hauling guano from Peru—even manure was better than no cargo at all.

Ultimately, the *Coeur de Lion* was sold to a German merchant, who sold her in 1860 to the Russian-American Fur Company. Under the Russian flag, she became the *Zaritza*, and paid a call in San Francisco. Nine years later, she cleared Newcastle, New South Wales, for Hong Kong, making the run in thirty-nine days. Some time in 1874 she went under the Swedish flag, and suffered the humiliation of being rerigged as a bark. World War I was raging in 1915 when the *Coeur de Lion* collided with another ship in the Baltic Sea and was lost—sixty-one years after her launching.

## *Emily Farnum*

SPECIFICATIONS: *Medium. Tonnage, 1,119. Length, 194 feet; breadth, 35 feet; depth, 23 feet. Owner, W. Jones & Co. of Portsmouth, N.H.*

**P**ROBABLY NO SAILING SHIP built on the Piscataqua is more familiar to local people than the medium size clipper, the *Emily Farnum*, because of the fine model of her that has been on display in Portsmouth Savings Bank for many years. She was named for a sister of the principal owner, William Jones. In addition to W. Jones & Company, which had five-eighths, Richard Jenness had one-quarter; and her master, Captain William Parker, one-eighth. She was launched July 1, 1854, and was the last clipper built on the Piscataqua in that year. She was described as "a fine freighting ship of about 1200 tons."[40] Her first voyage put her into the guano trade, which had become, as noted earlier, an occupation for clippers. Her cruise to the Chincha Islands was uneventful and she returned to Philadelphia in June, 1855. Loading at New York for San Francisco, she sailed on October 11, 1855, and arrived "previous to April 5,"[41] which would make her passage in excess of 160 days. She went on to Calcutta, and for a while was in the East Indies trade. However, the *Emily Farnum* found a place for herself in the history books on October 3, 1862.

On that day she attained a distinction not granted to many vessels: the *Emily Farnum* was captured and released by the Confederate raider, the *Alabama*. Not that the raider's captain, Raphael Semmes, wanted to be charitable—far from it. *Emily Farnum* had sailed from New York on September 21, 1862, under Captain Nathan Parker Simes. She was carrying an assorted cargo to Liverpool. The morning of October 3, latitude 40° north, longitude, 50° 30' west, roughly 300 miles southeast of Newfoundland, Captain Simes saw a vessel bearing down on him. When the stranger saw the American colors, she fired a warning shot, and ordered the *Emily Farnum* to heave to. With no chance of escaping the guns on the intercepting vessel, now flying the stars and bars, Captain Simes did as he was told. The Confederate captain sent over an officer with a boatload of armed sailors. The officer declared the *Emily Farnum* a prize of the warship *Alabama*, and ordered Simes to lower the American flag, which Simes refused to do, so the *Alabama*'s officer did it.

While this was going on, the *Alabama* went after another ship which had the misfortune of coming up over the horizon. She was the *Brilliant*, a transatlantic packet, and she also hove to. Captain Simes was ordered to take the *Emily Farnum*'s papers and go on board the *Alabama*.

*Among the prized possessions of the Portsmouth Athenaeum are these half models of four of Portsmouth's most famous clipper ships. From the top, they include the* Emily Farnum, Witch of the Wave, Sierra Nevada *and* Ocean Rover.

Captain Simes's private journal was later made available to William H.Y. Hackett, a Portsmouth lawyer who participated in the settling of the claims against the *Alabama*, long after the Civil War. Hackett said that Simes found a large number of prisoners, in irons, on the *Alabama*'s deck:

> ... The captain [Simes] was told to stand between two guns, and after long waiting on the deck, was ordered down to the cabin where he saw the captain of the *Alabama*, who was enjoying his cigar and wine, but unmindful of the forms of hospitality to his

visitor. He took Captain Simes' papers, and asked many questions about the ship, her cargo, owners, &c., and her value, where the cargo was owned, &c. Among the papers attached to a bill of lading was a certificate of the British consul in New York, showing that the goods on board were the property of John B. Spence, of Liverpool. When this was shown to Semmes, he declared it to be "bogus," and that it was "prepared by the owners for the purpose of saving their vessel."[42]

No matter Semmes's protestations of the validity of the certificate, there's little doubt that that piece of paper helped in saving her from destruction. Nevertheless, Semmes continued his cat-and-mouse game with Captain Simes for a while longer. He boasted of his captures; that he had burned eleven whalers off the Western Islands, and had put 190 prisoners on shore in that vicinity. He continued to question his prisoner about the movements of the opposing armies; how many vessels were being added to the U.S. Navy, and so on. Semmes let Simes know that he already had fifty-four prisoners on the *Alabama*, and had plenty more manacles for the *Emily Farnum*'s crew when the men came on board.

Finally Semmes tired of the game, and got down to business. After a conference with his clerk about the British consul's certificate, Semmes apparently decided that it would be impolitic to destroy British-owned property, so he asked Captain Simes if he would take all the prisoners then on the *Alabama*, plus the crew of the *Brilliant*, which vessel he planned to burn, and deliver them in Liverpool. Semmes spared no words in making it plain that he would rather have burned the *Emily Farnum*, but the logistics created by the prisoners, plus the technical questions raised by the consul's certificate, were inducing him to make the offer. It was quickly accepted by Captain Simes, who, after signing his parole, was allowed to return to his ship. The next day seventy-eight men were transferred to the *Emily Farnum*, being the captains, officers and crews of three vessels taken by the *Alabama*. As the *Emily Farnum*'s crew, with plenty of assistance, shook out her sails and got under way for Liverpool, a pall of smoke from the burning *Brilliant* blackened the horizon.

The *Emily Farnum* fared much better than two other Portsmouth-built vessels captured and burned by Confederate raiders. The stories of the *Express* and the *Shooting Star* will be told later. The third vessel destroyed was the *Rockingham*, but she was not a clipper and her tale will have to wait for another volume.

The *Emily Farnum* went about her business for her Portsmouth owners until 1872 when she was sold for $30,000 and was rerigged as a bark.[43] The object behind rerigging was simple: it reduced the number of hands needed to operate the vessel, and less overhead meant more profit from freights. In November, 1875, the *Emily Farnum* cleared San Francisco, heading for Departure Bay, Washington Territory. She ran into a gale the fifteenth, "which lasted 24 hours." The account continued:

> ...On the 18th the wind increased, accompanied by squalls and snow, and land was reported dead ahead. An attempt was at once made to stay the ship, which failed, and she was hauled to the wind, but, in endeavoring to weather Destruction Island, a heavy sea drove the vessel on the rocks, and at 12:30 she struck heavily...
>
> An effort was made to launch the boats, but they were destroyed by the force of the waves.... At 2:00 A.M. the vessel parted with the top part of her house, to which 14 men clung, lodging on the rocks, where they remained until morning. Thomas McGill swam from the rock to the main part of the island with a line, and a small raft was made and attached, by the means of which they reached shore two at a time. Before the raft, two of the men swam to the island, and John Hoaglin, a native of Sweden, and the Chinese were drowned in attempting the same feat. The survivors remained on the island for several days, living on flour and cabbage, until they were taken to the mainland by Indians.[44]

A chronometer reading, made prior to the wreck, showed the *Emily Farnum* as being thirty-five miles off shore, such was the limited reliability of navigational instruments at the time. In a letter from Port Townsend, Washington Territory, written in 1888, it was said: "Search is being made for the wreck of the bark *Emily Farnum*, which was lost 15 years ago. The vessel was laden with railroad iron for the Northern Pacific Railroad." To this was added the comment that neither the *Emily Farnum* "or her cargo of iron could be good for much after 15 years submersion in salt water."[45]

## Witch of the Wave (II)

SPECIFICATIONS: *Tonnage, 1,020. Length, 190 feet; breadth, 33.2 feet; depth, 22.1. Owners, Titcomb & Coffin, Newburyport, Mass.*

For THE FIRST TIME in the history of the Raynes Shipyard, the master was no longer on hand for the construction of a vessel. George Raynes might have been well enough to take part in the laying of the keel of the ship *Arkwright*, a non-clipper, but his death on April 12, 1855, left management in the hands of his son and partner, George Raynes, Jr. While George, Sr., might have known *Witch of the Wave* (II) was being planned, he had nothing to do with her construction. The second *Witch's* launching was scheduled for January 26, 1856, but weather brought a delay. *The Chronicle* reported:

> The beautiful ship *Witch of the Wave* was launched Monday afternoon in the midst of a cold snowstorm. If she proves as fast a sailer as her namesake, her owners cannot but be satisfied. The labors of the day closed with a sumptuous repast, for all hands employed on the ship, provided by Charles W. Walker, under the direction of the owners of the ship, Titcomb & Coffin. It is a noteworthy fact, no liquor was to be had on the premises.

To Frank Miller, publisher of *The Chronicle*, and an ardent temperance man, the fact no liquor was served was almost as important as the launching itself. But there's little doubt that Charles W. Walker, the proprietor of the Market House, on outer Market Street, near the shipyard, would have had a drop or two available in case some diner suffered indigestion. The launching also occasioned a poem by "Boiling Rock."[47]

> How gently, how smoothly the river she rides,
> Her model so graceful might cope with sea brides,
> With Apollo in beauty, with Hercules' strength—
> Her breadth and depth well compare with her length;
> Her finish will bear the keen critic's eye,
> Though bright as the stars in yon azure sky;
> Her constructor and workmen are of the right kind,
> As good as the best on the River you'll find.
> When fit for the ocean, she'll be a crack ship,
> May pay well her owners on every trip!
> And among the best ships in the world we may say,
> Are those built and launched on the Piscataqua.[46]

If nothing else, the poem does teach the reader that in the middle of the nineteenth century, Pis-cat-a-qua was pronounced Pis-cat-a-way, unless "Boiling Rock" was taking poetic license.

However, it was two months before the second *Witch* went to sea. *The Chronicle* reported on March 27, 1856, that besides the *Witch of the Wave*, "now lying at Pray's Wharf nearly ready for sea," Raynes & Son "have on the stocks, nearly ready for launch, a first class ship of about 1,000 tons [probably the *Annie Sise*], belonging to William F. Parrott of Boston. The reputation of the late George Raynes for building first class ships, is fully sustained by his son, the present builder, George Jr." A few days previously, *The Chronicle* had told of a mishap that shows the way in which boys played in the days of the Piscataqua clippers. Those splendid vessels must have been lodestones to youngsters: "On Friday afternoon on board the *Witch of the Wave*, a boy named Andrew Moran, twelve years old, fell from the deck into the hold, injuring him severely it is said; his skull being fractured and breaking one arm. Dr. [William] Laighton attended him. He is the son of John H. Moran," (a moulder who lived at 7 Brewster Street). So it is easy to see that boys from all over the recently chartered city used the new ships as playgrounds, no doubt against strict orders from their elders. Young Moran's fall was twenty-two feet.

Unfortunately, not much is known about the second *Witch*. While her predecessor attracted all kinds of publicity, *Witch* II cleared the Piscataqua a few days after the Moran incident, headed for Charleston, South Carolina, where she was to load with cotton. She took eleven days to make the passage, arriving April 6. When she left Charleston on May 2, she was carrying "3,335 bales of Upland cotton and 695 bags of Sea Island cotton, valued at $223,983, the most valuable cargo ever cleared from Charleston to Havre."[47] From Havre she went into the less glamorous and often odiferous guano trade. Funk & Wagnalls describes guano as "the accumulated excrement of sea birds found in the dry climate of the Peruvian coast and elsewhere...." The *Witch of the Wave* sailed to Callao, Peru, there to get the necessary papers that would permit her to go to the Chincha Islands to load guano. The sale of guano was a major source of revenue for the Peruvian government. Once loaded, the *Witch* headed back home. If the guano got wet while rounding the Horn, it became a rare delight to the nostrils as the vessel proceeded through the tropical zones.

The second *Witch* made one run to San Francisco, taking 135 days, which was twelve days longer than her namesake's slowest passage. However, weather could have been a factor—very little was certain in the days of sailing vessels. That run was in 1859, and with that she disappears from the pages of history. Quite possibly, the rampaging of Confederate cruisers during the Civil War induced Titcomb & Coffin to sell her to a foreign shipper.

## Shooting Star (II)

SPECIFICATIONS: Tonnage, 947. Length, 182 feet; breadth, 36,6 feet; depth, 23,6 feet. Owners, L. G. Hotchkiss, Gloucester, Mass.; E. M. Robinson, New Bedford; and S. G. Reed of Boston. Later, Reed, Wade & Co. of Boston.

To INCLUDE THE SECOND *SHOOTING STAR* in a roundup of clippers might be stretching a point. However, for the most part she was planned and built in the style of one, and by some experts she is labeled a "half-clipper." Because of the three-year gap between her launching in 1859, and that of the *Witch of the Wave*, it may be assumed that the Raynes yard was inactive, but that is far off the mark. After the *Witch*, the yard built and sent to sea four fair-sized, full-rigged ships, but they were not clippers; that fad had ended. These four Raynes vessels included the *Annie Sise* (1856), the *Jumna* (1856), the *Mary Washington* (1857), and the *Como* (1858). What prompted George Raynes, Jr., to try one more clipper is not known, because a change in shipbuilding was taking place, as related by Cutler:

> In a material sense the clipper ship era ended in 1857. No new clippers were launched thereafter in America. Ships of clipper form were built, it is true, fine smart-looking craft like the *Prima Donna* of Mystic, *Star of Peace*, at Newburyport, the *Industry* at Medford, the second *Mennon* at South Boston in 1858, and the second *Shooting Star* and the *Maid of the Sea* in 1859.
>
> They lacked, however, the lofty spars and immensely square yards of the clipper, having been planned at a time when the general reduction in the sail area of the older ships was under way.[48]

In the cases of at least two of Raynes's clippers, it has already been noted that their sail plans were reduced to convert them into barks. The *Coeur de Lion* and the *Wild Pigeon* come quickly to mind. Cutler stresses that in the case of the older clippers, it was not only an economy move but also one of safety. Hard-driving clipper captains like J. D. Whitmore had so strained the masts, spars and rigging that they were no longer safe, and the conversions did cut down on the manpower needed to sail them.

The *Shooting Star*'s namesake was one of the first clippers built in Medford, Massachusetts, launched in 1850 by James O. Curtis. The *Shooting Star* (II) made only one run to San Francisco in the less than spectacular time of 142 days, but there were worse runs than that on the record, even by the big, heavily rigged clippers, like the *Nightingale* and the *Sea Serpent*.

For the second *Shooting Star* there was the ignominious fate of being taken by a Confederate raider. The *Chickamauga* captured her on October 31, 1863, and burned her.

# III  *Fernald & Petigrew*

IF GEORGE RAYNES had ever been called upon to acknowledge his closest rival, he would undoubtedly have named Frederick Fernald. Certainly, those who have studied Piscataqua shipbuilding know that George Raynes and his son, George, Jr., had no patent on the art of building clipper ships. Fernald was eleven years younger than Raynes, but he died only a few days after the master. His partner, William Petigrew (to use the spelling of the time) lived to a ripe old age, dying in 1892.

Oddly, both Fernald and Petigrew had been associated early in their careers with men named Raynes. Petigrew had been a master workman in the Raynes Shipyard before forming a partnership with Fernald in 1844. Fernald started out alone as a shipbuilder. Where he served his apprenticeship is not clear, but in 1835, at the age of twenty-four, Fernald built and launched the 448-ton *Harriet Rockwell*. That was in a yard at the foot of Pickering Street in Portsmouth, which was sited approximately where the Piscataqua Marine Laboratory is now. It is hard to believe, looking at the site at the present day, that vessels of any size could be launched there, but they were.[1] Fernald was five years younger than George Raynes had been when the latter launched his first vessel, the *Planet*. Fernald named the *Harriet Rockwell* in honor of his wife. In that same location, he built the still larger *Thomas Perkins*, and a news item of May 27, 1837, hinted at events to come:

> A fine ship was launched from the yard of John Mugridge, near the South Mill Bridge, on Tuesday [May 23]. It's probably the longest merchant ship ever built on this river, being 157 feet long, but very narrow (only 31 feet), calculated for fast sailing. The ship

67

is well built and is highly creditable to the master carpenter Frederick W. Fernald.

Exactly where Fernald obtained the plans and model for such a vessel is not known. It was a radical size, being five times as long as it was wide—the same proportions of many of the clippers. Possibly a Boston designer produced the plans. The late Gertrude Pickett, who had access to the Fernald and Petigrew papers, which are now in the Peabody Museum in Salem, Massachusetts, made no reference to Fernald's early training. The *Thomas Perkins* was his last vessel in the one-time Mugridge yard.[2] In 1837, Fernald made his move to Badger's Island where he took over the yard that had been founded by William Badger. Others had occupied the yard after Badger's death in 1830. Charles Cushing was one, and he built the *Fortitude* there at the same time Fernald was constructing the *Harriet Rockwell*. Fernald's first vessel on Badger's Island, in the state of Maine, was the first *New Hampshire*, 593 tons. Shortly after that, Fernald entered into a partnership with Charles Raynes. Not much is known of Charles Raynes's background, but the city directories describe him as a shipbuilder.[3] The first venture for the firm of Raynes & Fernald was the 600-ton *Columbia* and one of her owners was Samuel Hale of Somersworth, from whom the partners had leased the Badger Shipyard. That partnership lasted until 1844, when they split up, and Fernald became associated with William Petigrew, a partnership that lasted until Fernald's untimely death on April 30, 1855, at the age of forty-four. They produced twenty-four three-masted ships, seven of which were clippers, one bark, one brig and four schooners in their eleven years.[4]

Many of the workmen who were in the yards of other builders at various times also worked for Fernald & Petigrew. Shipbuilding was a business with many specialties, and the journeymen went where their trades were in demand at any given time. No doubt men like William L. Fernald, later a shipbuilder himself in the former Raynes Shipyard, was employed there. As was William Fry, who died July 25, 1891, in his East Eliot home. Fry's obituary said, in part, "He was also employed in Fernald & Petigrew's yard on Badger's Island."[5] However, for one of the special crafts, carving, Fernald & Petigrew went outside the Piscataqua region to get their work done. "In the art of carving there was no contract, but a bill was rendered on completion of the work. Most of the carving for the Fernald & Petigrew ships was done by S. W. Gleason & Sons...of Commercial St., Boston."[6]

Fernald already had one vessel of more than a thousand tons to his credit when he formed the partnership with Petigrew. The *Empire*, 1,049 tons, was bought by D. and A. Kingsland of New York. When the

*Fernald family tombstone is adjacent to the Raynes family tombstone in Union cemetery, Portsmouth, New Hampshire. Author's photograph.*

Fernald and Petigrew partnership came into being, Fernald carefully worded a letter to the Kingslands, dated January 18, 1845:

> I take the liberty of writing to you and state I have taken in as a co-partner Mr. William Petigrew (formerly master workman for George Raynes). We are now building a ship for Messers Shepherd and Marcy of 150 feet long, 33 feet beam. She will be launced in May or June next. She is about framed out.
> If you or any of your friends should think of building a ship this season we are ready to make a contract to get one off in the early fall ....[7]

The vessel on the ways was the *Judah Touro*, named for a close business associate of the Marcy brothers, Daniel and Peter. Judah Touro hailed from Newport, Rhode Island, where his name is still held in reverence, but he and Peter Marcy were then residents of New Orleans. Daniel Marcy took the *Judah Touro* to sea. Another ship for which Fernald and Petigrew contracted was the *R. D. Shepherd*, 795 tons, named in honor of still another Marcy associate. Fernald and Petigrew also became involved with the Tucker family of Wiscasset, Maine. For them they built the *Samoset*, a freighter that went into the cotton trade. In January, 1847, they agreed with the Kingslands for the construction of the ship *Columbus*, which, at 1,307 tons, was the first on the river to exceed 1,300 tons. Then came the *Danube*, 749 tons; the *Peter Marcy*, 821 tons. The Kingslands ordered a sister ship to the *Columbus*, which was launched in 1849 as the *Empire State*. The *Western World*, a passenger packet of 1,354 tons, was built in 1850, also for the Kingslands. Late in 1850, again for the Kingslands, the partnership began its first clipper, the *Typhoon*.

# Typhoon

SPECIFICATIONS: *Extreme. Tonnage, 1,612. Length, over all, 225 feet; keel, 207 feet; breadth, 42.5 feet; depth, 23 feet. Owners, Daniel and Ambrose Kingsland.*

**W**HEN THE *TYPHOON* was launched on February 18, 1851, she was the largest merchant vessel yet built on the Piscataqua. It is possible to get an idea of her size by comparison to the oldest sailing ship afloat— the *USS Constitution*. "Old Ironsides" displaces 2,200 tons, but the *Typhoon* was twenty-one feet longer over all. Although the Kingslands had contracted for a fast clipper, it is of note that already their thinking was turning to steam. On October 8, 1850, they wrote:

> We are yet undetermined whether we shall put machinery into the ship, but should like to have her framed in such a manner that we can do so if we are so disposed.[8]

Fortunately for the story of the Piscataqua clippers, the Kingslands finally decided that they were not "disposed" toward making the *Typhoon* a steamer. While they were mulling it over, work began in November, following the lines of a model which had already been approved. The plans had been drafted by Samuel Pook of Boston, and Fernald obtained them through friends on the Navy Yard. The launching was dramatically described in *The Portsmouth Journal*, February 22, 1851:

> We have witnessed the launching of many superb ships on the Piscataqua, but never before one so beautiful and in some respects so novel as the launch of the splendid ship *Typhoon* from the yard of Messers. Fernald and Petigrew, on Tuesday, 18th inst. This ship is a model of the architectural beauty of our mercantile marine, and the ability and skill of her enterprising builders. Full rigged on the stocks, with the masts and yards all aloft, her gay colors displayed and floating in the breeze of a bright and mild winter day, she stood like a bride adorned for her wedding. At the precise time appointed, half past 12 o'clock, without the sound of an axe or a hammer being heard (battering rams being used for driving the wedges), she glided slowly with the ease of a Queen into the water, and sat with all the graceful beauty of a swan upon its surface, floating in the mid-channel of the river, and as with the still flowing tide, she swung around and brought up safely at her anchor with no shock or concussion which would have broken a pipe stem, a murmur of gratification and delight ran through

*Typhoon, off Liverpool after her record run from Portsmouth, New Hampshire. Painting by Samuel Walters. Portsmouth Athenaeum collection.*

the crowds which covered the wharves and female beauty which filled every window of opposite buildings.

The builders gave an elegant entertainment to their friends at the Rockingham House on the afternoon of the launch, at which time there was a gentle zephyr of good feeling, no small breeze of mirth, and a typhoon of wit and sentiment.

Messers. Fernald & Petigrew, the very enterprising builders of *Typhoon*, have within a few years done a gigantic business. They have made a *Western World*, and a *Columbus* to sail after it. They have launched a *Germania*, and set afloat the *Danube*. The *Granite State* [a schooner] they have put in sailing trim, and sent the *Empire State* across the ocean. But their last effort is the crowner of the whole—to put to the test they have now launched a *Typhoon* to compass the world.

*The Journal's* editor, Charles Brewster, really could wax eloquent when he chose, then, in the next sentence or two change his pace into straight prose as he did in describing *Typhoon*, right down to the fact that her "treenails [trunnel is a variation] are of the best Long Island locust." For most modern readers, the specifications given, and the descriptions, and terminology, are about as comprehensible as would be an essay on the internal workings of a jet aircraft engine. But Brewster's account of the living quarters for the crew, officers and passengers can be easily accepted in present-day terms:

...She has a small top-gallant forecastle, sufficiently large however for practible purposes, house on deck, abaft foremast, 40 feet long, 15 feet wide, fitted for galleys, sail room, carpenter and boatswain, and entrances to the between decks. She has a house in front of the poop deck to protect entrance to the cabin, 12 feet square, beautifully finished. You first enter the second cabin which is finished, for officers—pantry, storerooms, &c., to be handsomely grained. Passing through this, you enter the main Cabin or saloon; and here we must stop for words to describe the skill of our worthy mechanics. In richness and beauty it surpasses everything heretofore attempted. It is of pine, white enameled, and it can only be compared to the best of china for purity of texture; it is magnificently relieved with gilt ornaments, and it is to be furnished in a manner worthy of the finest *boudoir* in the country. The State Rooms, seven in number, are very large and airy, and are to be splendidly furnished. She has two skylights for lighting the cabin, securely protected. The Forecastle for sailors is under deck forward; is very large and airy, every attention having been paid for the comfort of poor Jack—it being unequalled by any ship afloat; it is amply large for 40 men.

Resplendent as the *Typhoon* no doubt was, she was but the beginning of the rush to extravagant passenger apartments and furnishings. After her launching, the *Typhoon* was nearly ready for sea, and Captain Charles H. Salter, one of the many young shipmasters native to Portsmouth, made ready to sail. Captain Salter was only twenty-seven, but already he had commanded the Raynes-built *Venice* at the age of twenty-two. Captain Salter took the *Typhoon* to sea on March 12, 1851, after a down-river tow by the *R. B. Forbes*. Her maiden passage was unusual in that she cleared directly from Portsmouth for Liverpool, sailing in ballast. Captain Salter took her across in thirteen days, ten hours, still a record for sail between Portsmouth and Liverpool. Jubilantly, the owners informed the builders on April 11:

> By letter received from Capt. Salter we are informed of his safe arrival out to Liverpool .... on the morning of the 26th, thus making the passage in 13½ days from dock to dock. Capt. Salter and also his cabin passengers will no doubt have advised you by the same mail that brought our letters of the splendid run of the ship. We notice complimentary notice of her in the Liverpool paper and this morning our papers have generally noticed the passage as extraordinary ....[9]

The excitement that the *Typhoon's* record-making run created in Liverpool was reported by *The New York Express*, and reprinted by *The Portsmouth Journal:*

> Great Passage—The new American clipper ship *Typhoon*, Capt. Salter, which sailed from Portsmouth on the 12th ult. arr. off Holyhead on the 25th ult. and at her wharf the next morning, thus accomplishing the passage dock to dock in 13½ days, including calm and head winds .... She has been visited by hundreds of admiring spectators, says *The Liverpool Times* ....

Why the *Typhoon* went directly to Liverpool, with little or no freight and only three persons described as passengers, is not clear. Supposedly she was carrying a strongbox of gold to the owners' Liverpool correspondents, and it is possible there was cargo waiting for her there. Two Exeter, New Hampshire, men, John Lowe and George Gardner, were on board. Edward F. Sise was described both as a passenger and as supercargo.[10] Judging from a letter Sise wrote to Fernald and Petigrew, the latter description is probably appropriate. In much of what he said, Sise did not indulge himself in any civic pride. One of his complaints was that the *Typhoon* went to sea shorthanded; there were only thirty men and boys to do the work, and many had never been to sea before. It was Sise's opinion that she might have made the run in eleven or twelve days had she had experienced hands. But it is hard to understand Sise's criticism because he must have known, as well as anyone, that getting a full crew for a clipper in Portsmouth, at that time, was well nigh impossible. The *Typhoon* also experienced rough weather:

> ... We had one dreadful night — was struck by lightning twice, but thank God we escaped. The marks are left in many places in our beautiful cabin ....[11]

It seems almost callous of Sise that he could deplore the damage to the cabin interior without mentioning the real tragedy that took place during the lightning storm:

> The *Typhoon* left Portsmouth on the 12th ult. On the morning of the 16th, while all hands were on deck, taking in sail, Mr. Kingsbury was disabled by a fall, the decks being slippery with ice. On the same day, says our correspondent, a severe gale, accompanied by thunder and lightning, was experienced. William P. Badger, one of the hands, from New Hampshire, was struck by lightning, making a hole in his oil cloth top coat the size of an ounce ball, setting his underclothing on fire; he was badly burned from his shoulder to his feet, the fluid running down his back. On the arrival of the vessel at Liverpool he was taken to the hospital. The lightning struck the ship a second time, passed into the after cabin, making visible marks on the gilding, and passed off without damage to the ship or passengers. On the 17th passed an iceberg, lat 42° 50', lon 48° 30' [A few miles south of Newfoundland.]

The above report in *The Boston Journal*, as reprinted by *The Portsmouth Journal*, was certainly much more in balance than that of the arrogant, youthful Edward Sise. The injured youth was William P. Badger of Newmarket, and he died from his injuries in a Liverpool hospital a week later at the age of nineteen.[12]

Sise exulted in the accolades accorded the *Typhoon*, "Hundreds have hailed her today .... she is greatly admired by all who have seen her and should be surprised if she was sold here as parties have asked the lowest price for her ...." He added his personal thoughts:

> Well now after praising her she has some defects. In the first place the Iron work is constantly breaking — and certainly must be bad, I have seen it break .... You and Knowlton [John, Portsmouth blacksmith] as well as some New York work will catch it from Salter — he has a bucket full.
> Again she leaks very badly, and has never been freed without one hour's pumping in each watch, which has completely disheartened some of our best men. One night I went out and six men were sitting down by the pumps and told me they were really

beat out. So many have been on board today that she has not been pumped out and Captain Salter did remark that she had three feet of water in her hold ....[13]

Captain Salter apparently waited until the dockyard gates were closed before doing any pumping. He was not about to let the *Typhoon*'s English admirers know that she was a sailing sieve. No matter what her maiden passage woes, the *Typhoon* went round to London and, moored in the Thames, she attracted thousands of viewers, most of them seeing their first American clipper, and the largest afloat at that time. Shortly thereafter, she left London, and recrossed to New York. On August 2, 1851, she sailed on the first of her two passages to San Francisco, arriving in the relatively good time of 108 days. Of the Piscataqua-built clippers, only the *Dashing Wave* and the *Sierra Nevada* surpassed it. Throughout the passage, she was in a race with the *Raven* and the *Sea Witch*. The *Typhoon* was first into San Francisco, but the *Raven*, right behind her, was declared the winner because she had left Boston five days after the *Typhoon* left New York. Across the Pacific the *Typhoon* went, and into Calcutta in seventy-nine days. Heading for London, she ran from Calcutta to the Cape of Good Hope in thirty-seven days, a record tied by the *Witch of the Wave* a year later, but never beaten. Her Calcutta-London time was 107 days. *The Chronicle* reported on December 9, 1852, "We learned that a telegraphic dispatch was received in this city last evening, from New York, announcing the arrival of the clipper *Typhoon*, Capt. Salter, in 23 days from Liverpool. This is a remarkably fast run for the season." On her next voyage around the world, the *Typhoon* suffered a mishap in San Francisco Harbor when she ran up on a rock. She had to be beached for repairs at Teneon Point:

> It is a novel sight to see the clipper ship *Typhoon* lying flat on her side at a wharf, with her vast spars hanging like the boughs of a tree over the heads of the passersby, and touching the eaves of a warehouse. The curious spectacle causes a universal halt to both the idle and the busy. But there she is, lying just as snugly as though in her natural position — a steam pump in a lighter is puffing away to relieve her of the water she has taken in, while on the other side is a swarm of busy workmen running along under keel, and hammering at her seams, and replacing the copper to keep the same element out. *Typhoon* requires to be hove over on both sides; have the copper on the larboard side stripped; false keel refastened and repairs made permanent.[14]

When finally repaired, the *Typhoon* resumed her passage to load tea at Shanghai. Once loaded and cleared, she was 104 days to London.

Her run home to New York was much smoother than the one she endured in the late winter of 1857:

> ... Has had very bad weather, since 1st inst. On the 3rd, under close-reefed topsails, she was in a hurricane for eight hours. It blew two topsails away, blew her rigging, leaving mainmast a complete wreck ... On the 14th a block fell, killing a passenger named J. Seddons, badly cutting a sailor's head. Out of a crew of 40 men, but 10 were left to do ship's duty.[15]

Refitted for sails and other running gear, the *Typhoon* was entered in the hotly competitive tea trade between the East Indies, China and England. With the outbreak of the Civil War shipping went into a decline, and the *Typhoon* was reported as disengaged in Singapore in 1863. The Kingslands sold her to a British firm when the *CSS Alabama* set up a blockade. She had cost $55,000 to build, and they sold her for $39,000, not a bad deal for the Kingslands, when all the profit she had made for them over a dozen years is considered.[16] Captain Salter stayed with her, at least until 1865 when, in May, she was at Hong Kong from Saigon. In 1869 she was registered as the British ship the *Indomitable*. It is believed that the *Typhoon* was lost, appropriately enough, in a typhoon in the China Sea in 1871.

The *Typhoon's* first master, Charles H. Salter, is worthy of more than passing mention. He was one of the great clipper captains and respected as such. The family had a sea-faring tradition almost as ancient as Davy Jones's Locker. And Captain Salter did leave behind him a record that has never been challenged — his run to Liverpool in 1851. When he left ship's command, Salter became superintendent of Pacific Mail Steamship Company's dock in San Francisco, but gave that up because of ill health.[17] A few years later he went back to the Pacific coast and resumed the post. In 1879, he came east for good, and for a while made his home on his farm in Greenland, New Hampshire, but was resident in Portsmouth when he died on September 28, 1884, about the age of seventy.

*The Chronicle* said of him:

> Capt. Salter was reputed a thorough seaman and most efficient officer and commander; was cordial and agreeable in his intercourse with his fellow citizens, and enjoyed their respect and esteem to a very large extent.

A painting of the *Typhoon* by Samuel Walters, an English artist, was presented to the Portsmouth Athenaeum by the Salter family, and still hangs there.

## Red Rover

SPECIFICATIONS: *Extreme. Tonnage, 1,021. Length, 172 feet; breadth, 35 feet; depth, 23 feet. Owner, Robert L. Taylor & Co.*

LIKE SOME OTHER PISCATAQUA CLIPPERS, the *Red Rover* never became a household name. Launched on October 27, 1852, she promptly had a bit of trouble. After she had gone down the ways, she collided with a Canadian schooner, the *McEllan*, inbound from Windsor, Nova Scotia, with a cargo of plaster. The *Red Rover* escaped serious harm, only breaking off a davit, but was then further damaged when she crashed into a dock. The collision, however, did little to dampen the spirits of the day, when a collation was served in the Market House.[18] Ichabod Goodwin, who would become New Hampshire's first Civil War governor, was the owner's agent in supervising construction. Captain William O. Putnam, formerly of the ship *Ambassador*, was commander.

The *Red Rover* had one more mishap before leaving Portsmouth, never to return. A few days after her launching, while being masted and sparred for sea, workmen were engaged in placing her mizzen topmast. It had been hoisted and belayed "when a laborer, by some unaccountable blunder, cast off the rope, and the top mast came down on the run, bruising and splitting the deck beam, and then fell over the rail, breaking off. No one was hurt."[19]

The *Red Rover* sailed on November 24, 1852, with a stiff northwest breeze behind her, headed for New York and, ultimately, China. Late in December, she cleared New York for San Francisco, and *The Chronicle* proudly echoed word from New York that she was "the finest of her type in port. Judging from her remarkable run to that port, although encountering one of the worst storms of the season, she should have a short run to San Francisco." Foul weather, shortly after leaving New York, and a hard time rounding the Horn, kept the *Red Rover* from any record. Her time was 117 days, which was not disgraceful. The *Red Rover* made four more round-the-world voyages to San Francisco, and her times to that port averaged out to the fastest of any of the Piscataqua-built clippers—116½ days. Her best was 109 days, beaten only by the *Typhoon* and the *Sierra Nevada;* she equalled the times of the *Sea Serpent* and the *Wild Pigeon*.

She returned from her first voyage in time to be in New York when Donald McKay's masterpiece, the 4,000-ton clipper, the *Great Republic*, was destroyed by a fire that started in a waterfront bakeshop. Early

*Red Rover off Holy Head after a twelve day voyage from New York. The Mariners Museum collection.*

reports in Portsmouth were to the effect that the *Red Rover* had been burned to the water's edge. These proved untrue, although the *Red Rover* suffered some damage. The total damage from the fire was estimated at $1.5 million. The *Red Rover* was repaired, and left on her second westward voyage on January 22, 1854, a journey of 120 days. After unloading in San Francisco, she went to Callao, Peru, to get her licenses to load guano in the Chincha Islands. It may have been at that time that one of her officers had problems with Peruvian officials. Whatever happened, other shipmasters and officers memorialized Congress, asking for a protest. These memorials were posted, for signature, in the Portsmouth Athenaeum, a rendezvous for nautical people in those days, and also in the Exchange Building Reading Room.

The *Red Rover* went about her voyages to San Francisco. On her fourth, three days out of New York, she was tossed on her beam ends, and suffered heavy damage. "The cargo shifted and thereafter she had a list of three strakes [each strake the width of a hull plank] which materially lessened her speed when sailing with starboard tacks aboard."[20] Despite that mishap, she made it to San Francisco in 112 days. Her return was via the guano islands to Havre and then to New York. The fifth voyage went without incident until she arrived at London, where she went adrift and grounded, whereupon a German steamer plowed into her. The damages put her into Victoria Dock for repairs. In 1860, she was overhauled in New York, and then sold to James Baines & Company, Limited, of Liverpool and Brisbane, for $25,000 and became the *Young Australia*. The Baines firm used her as a packet in its Black Ball Line, sailing between Liverpool and Australia. She long held her sailing qualities as shown by a letter written in 1892 by a former captain:

> I had the honor of being chief officer of the *Cairngorm* in 1860-61, and left her to take command of the American-built clipper ship *Young Australia*. In 1862, the *Stornaway* left Sydney for London and about one day later I left Melbourne with the *Young Australia*, also for London, via Cape Horn. Both these vessels belonged to the same employ, Viz Liverpool Black Ball Line. In the South Atlantic I overtook *Stornaway* and on actual recognition we both did our best to outstrip one another. This lasted (within sight of each other) for about 10 days when we parted company in the night and I had the satisfaction of arriving at destination (London) about two days earlier than *Stornaway*. The *Young Australia* referred to above was previously named *Red Rover*.
>
> Wm. Lowrie[21]

When the Baines Company fell on hard times late in the 1860s, the

Red Rover *after her name had been changed to* Young Australia. *National Maritime Museum, San Francisco, collection.*

*Young Australia* was sold to J. P. Foulks and homeported in Liverpool. Working her way out of Moreton Bay, four hours out of Brisbane, on a homeward passage, she went on the rocks of Moreton Island on May 31, 1872.

*Water Witch flying the house flag of S. Tilton. Painting by J. E. Buttersworth, circa 1853. Peabody Museum of Salem collection.*

## Water Witch

SPECIFICATIONS: *Tonnage, 1,204. Length, 178 feet—over all, 192; breadth, 38.25 feet; depth, 21 feet; 7.75 feet between decks. Owners, Stephen Taylor, et al, of Boston.*

THE *WATER WITCH* never had a chance to live up to the high hope held for her because her career was too short. But what a sight she must have been as she sat on the stocks on May 7, 1853, waiting for the long slide into the water. Her ways, on the northwesterly end of Badger's Island, were upriver a few hundred yards from Samuel Badger's yard on Kittery Foreside, and Badger's workmen no doubt stopped their tasks to watch the performance of a friendly rival.[22] Farther down river, workmen at the Portsmouth Navy Yard, ever glad for an opportunity to drop their tools, used the noon hour to be spectators. A published account said:

> The noble clipper ship *Water Witch* of 1200 tons burthen, fully masted on the stocks, will be launched from the yard of Fernald & Petigrew this day at 12 o'clock. She is owned in Boston, and will be commanded by Capt. Washington Plumer of this town.[23]

Two days later it was reported:

> The clipper ship *Water Witch* was launched promptly at the appointed time, 12 o'clock Saturday in fine style. The ship was fully coppered and masted on the stocks, being dressed in festoons of flags and parti-colored signals from truck to rail. The Union Jack at the bowsprit, at the fore truck, the ship's name in Boston numbers, at the main a pennant, and a complete set of Marryat's signals; at the mizzen the American ensign.[24]

After launching, fully rigged and waiting to sail, the *Water Witch* was lying at a wharf, and one report said that standing on "one of our wharves on Wednesday, the observer could see four new ships on the stocks."[25] Portsmouth's waterfront was a busy place in the 1850s, as the "Old Town by the Sea" cashed in on the frenzy for West Coast development. The clippers, and other square-riggers built at the same period, created a prosperity almost unequalled in Piscataqua annals. The *Water Witch*'s builders had already laid the keel for her sister, the *Dashing Wave*. On June 20, 1853, the *Water Witch* left the fast-running river to keep her date with destiny:

> The fine clipper ship *Water Witch*, built by Messers. Fernald & Petigrew, and commanded by Capt. Washington Plumer, sailed from this port on Saturday forenoon. A steam tug was engaged to tow her around, but not arriving, she started alone. When off Frost's Point, she was met and taken in tow by the steamer; but instead of towing the ship, it was required all the speed of the boat to prevent her being run down by the clipper—so the tow line was cast off and the ship allowed to proceed. She had nothing but topsails set as the towboat was expected to carry her around. An open house was held on the *Water Witch* before sailing and many viewed the spacious cabin.[26]

Boston newspapers were ecstatic over the *Water Witch*, and detailed reports describing her were published, after her arrival without the benefit of the tug:

> ... She has long sharp ends, but rounded load lines, and is without head boards, A female figure in flowing vestments, tastefully bronzed, ornaments the bow, and on either side of the cutwater the angles are filled with gilded carved work, embracing her name. Although her bow rises gently, yet her sheer is graduated her whole length, and is as true as the curve of a circle. Her stern is oval in outline, and is elaborately ornamented with carved work, embracing a scene with three water witches in the center.
> ... Her bulwarks are 5 feet 4 inches high, including the monkey rail, and are built solid, like those of a ship of war; are clamped inside and out .... She has a topgallant forecastle and abaft the foremast a large house, which contains accommodations for the crew, the galley, quarters for her boys, and other apartments. Her cabin is built into a half-poop deck, and has two entrances, one forward and the other aft, the latter leading to the poop where she is steered. The after-cabin contains five state-rooms, and other apartments, and is beautifully wainscotted with mahogany, rosewood, and bird's-eye maple, relieved with gilded mouldings and flowers ....
> The ship herself is built of the best materials, in the first style of workmanship. Her keel is of rock maple in two depths .... Her floor ceiling is four inches thick ....
> Her frame is of New Hampshire white oak, well seasoned, her upper wales, and also her chain bolt strakes, are of oak, and the rest of her planking and ceiling are of hard pine. She is seasoned with salt.
> ... Her builders are well known as among the most thorough and experienced mechanics in the country ... She is not only beautiful and well built, but we believe will prove a remark-

ably fast sailer ... All who have inspected her, speak of her in the highest terms ... She lies at the south side of Lewis wharf, call and see her.[27]

When the writer observed that the *Water Witch* was "seasoned with salt," he was touching one of the key points in understanding why well built wooden ships, particularly their hulls, could last so long. Many writers discussing ships mention them as being seasoned with salt, an ancient practice brought to America by the earliest English shipwrights. The technique of seasoning against dry rot was as follows:

> ... The process is to wash the timbers by means of a syringe with strong brine and then fill the spaces between them from the gunwale to the turn of the bilge with rock or common rough salt and if the first dose is administered effectually, it seldom requires repetition for the incipient fungus is usually destroyed once and forever.[28]

However, no matter how well "seasoned" a vessel might be, fending off ill fortune was almost impossible. The *Water Witch* seemed to exist under an evil star. On her first passage from Boston to San Francisco, she had to put into Rio de Janeiro, almost a wreck. A storm had dismasted her, and she had four feet of water in her hold when she made port. All the cargo had to be offloaded and dried out while the *Water Witch* underwent repairs. In total time, her first passage to San Francisco spanned 228 days; it was not the worst on record, however. After unloading, the *Water Witch* sailed south along the American coasts to the Chincha Islands where she loaded with guano, and arrived at Hampton Roads, Virginia, in sixty-four days, six of which were spent getting around the Horn. She headed back to San Francisco on December 6, 1854, and arrived on April 11, 1855. Her orders then directed her to Mazatlan on the Pacific coast of Mexico to load dye-wood for New York. The first accounts of her loss in a gale also reported Captain Plumer as a drowning victim. A later news item in *The Boston Chronicle* had the *Water Witch* valued at $68,000 plus her freight money of $24,000, all of which was insured. The hope was expressed that Captain Plumer had survived.[29]

Plumer's letter to the owners, reporting the wreck, confirmed the safety of himself and his crew, although they escaped with only the clothes they were wearing. Plumer said she dragged her anchors in the gale, then struck a hidden rock, after which she went to pieces. Wreckers paid $500 for what remained of a once-promising vessel.[30]

## Dashing Wave

*SPECIFICATIONS: Medium clipper. Tonnage, 1,239. Length, 184.3; breadth, 38.2; depth, 19.1. Owners, Stephen Tilton Co.*

**I**F THE *DASHING WAVE* had no other claim to a heroic place in the annals of both Piscataqua and American clippers, her long life would assure her of it. With only the very probable exception of the clipper *Syren*, another New Englander, she was the last of the clippers in any kind of sea-going service, and she might have been still under sail as late as 1910. The Piscataqua shipwrights built their vessels to last, and before the *Dashing Wave* ended her career sixty-seven years after launching, she had passed through a myriad of adventures.

As indicated in the account of the *Water Witch*, Fernald & Petigrew was a substantial, fast-moving partnership. They apparently had built up enough financial wherewithal of their own to begin construction of another clipper, while finishing the *Water Witch*, with the sanguine expectations that a buyer would come along, and they were not disappointed. Such was the aura of success that was attending the operation of Fernald and Petigrew that *The Chronicle*, on July 15, 1853, gave quite a bit of its limited news space to the *Dashing Wave*:

> According to previous notice, the beautiful clipper ship *Dashing Wave* was launched yesterday afternoon at 5 o'clock from the yard of Fernald & Petigrew. This ship is of the same model as *Water Witch*, which was launched a few weeks ago. She is thoroughly built, copper fastened, sheathed with yellow metal to her deep load lines.
>
> After the launching, a collation was given by Capt. Ichabod Goodwin and F&P, the owners of the ship, on which occasion, the following sentiment was offered by William H. Y. Hackett and recived with rapturous applause:
>
> "Our friends, Messers. Fernald & Petigrew — Their ingenuity, enterprise, and liberality is without bounds; in former days they were content, like the rest of us, to make little *Catherines* or *Elizas*, but they soon changed the *Fashion* and show our New York friends a *Columbus*. They have caused the *Danube* to run, and created an *Empire State*. They have made a *Western World* and a *Frank Pierce* to sail it, and even compelled a *Levi Woodbury* to walk the plank; and, having created a beautiful *Water Witch*, they now send an elegant *Dashing Wave* to roll its builders' fame to the Pacific shores."

*Dashing Wave entering Boston Harbor; Boston Light in the background. Painting by William Bradford. Mark Sexton photograph. Peabody Museum of Salem collection.*

By August 30, the *Dashing Wave* had been sold to the same concern that had bought the *Water Witch*. "We are informed also that Fernald & Petigrew have laid the keels of two new ships, one a freighter, 1,025 tons, on their own account; the other a clipper of 900 for parties in Boston."[31]

The *Dashing Wave*, under Captain John D. Fiske, left the Piscataqua "of and for Boston," Sept. 27, and arrived there the next day. She was sent on to Philadelphia, from whence she sailed to San Francisco, November 25, 1853. Gertrude Pickett conceded that the *"Dashing Wave has no claim to a spectacular career, but she will be remembered for her endurance, and for her long life of service."*[32] She took 118 days to San Francisco, which was far from disgraceful, and then made a good run from there to Calcutta, besting the clippers *Polynesia*, *Syren* and *Westward-Ho*. Captain Fiske also took the *Dashing Wave* on her second world voyage, reaching San Francisco in 122 days; she returned via Cape Horn to New York.

In 1858, under a Captain Young, she made her best San Francisco passage — 107 days. Other than a run by Tobey & Littlefield's *Sierra Nevada*, that was the best time ever achieved by a Piscataqua clipper, and it was more than respectable. In all, the *Dashing Wave* made six runs to the Golden Gate, her longest being 141 days, her average, 121. The *Dashing Wave* experienced many mishaps, as did most of the clippers. Some of her adventures are related below:

> After leaving Calcutta, June 1, 1857, she grounded in the river, and had to put back with four feet of water in the hold; the cargo was discharged and she was in port two months before resuming her voyage. In December, 1864, she was at Singapore repairing damages sustained on her passage from Hong Kong .... She was at Barnegat, the night of Feb. 8, 1867, and struck on the shoals and got off leaking badly. Off Woodlands she received her pilot .... all hands at the pumps and the leak gaining, when up to the point of Sandy Hook, a tug hooked on but at 1 P.M. had to leave her. At 7 p.m. she sank in five fathoms, the main deck being five feet under water. The officers and crew were taken off by the tug. She remained under water until Sept. 12 when she was raised and towed to New York. She was then valued at $76,000 .... On her last passage from New York, she sailed March 11, 1869 and was 42 days to 50 degrees south in the Atlantic [the latitude of Cape Horn]; then had a succession of gales, during which she lost spars, split sails and started a bad leak. Captain Mayhew was sick and the ship was put about for Rio, arriving July 6. There she discharged part of her cargo and repaired at a cost of $37,000, left port Oct. 11 and when again off Cape Horn encountered heavy gales and started a new leak. Steered for Valparaiso, arriving

there Dec. 5, Captain Mayhew being very sick; the mate, Morton, being in charge and the crew mutinous. The captain was taken ashore and died Dec. 10. The leak was found to be in the bottom of the vessel and was repaired by divers . . . . reached San Francisco, Feb. 15, 341 days from New York.[33]

The above account, especially the last part, is at variance with reported times. But it is hard to find authorities agreeing on the times of sailing vessels.

The *Dashing Wave* had many owners in the course of a long life. In 1870, she was registered to G. D. S. Trask, with New York as her hailing port. When she arrived in San Francisco after the long passage related above, she was modified for service as a lumber hauler, working out of Puget Sound, usually south to San Francisco which was still going through the growing pains brought on by gold fever. A news item reported, December 12, 1883:

> *Dashing Wave*, 1054 tons register, which was built at this port in 1853, is now owned in Tacoma, Wash. Terr., and has for some years been successfully employed in the coal trade between San Francisco and the coal ports on the northern Pacific coast of the U.S. Not long since, the ship was inspected, and, although 30 years old, was found to be worth thorough repairs which she received at Tacoma. While the work was in progress, a six-pound cannon ball was found solidly embedded in the wood, it having remained there ever since it was fired into her in the War of the Rebellion as she was leaving the harbor of Galveston, Texas, with a cargo of cotton on board.[34]

A few months later, there was another report on the *Dashing Wave*, quoting *The San Francisco Call:*

> Ship *Dashing Wave*, Capt. Connor, arrived in port from Tacoma with 650,000 feet of lumber. This old ship was built in 1853, and four years later came out to this coast, and for many years afterward plied between here and Eastern ports. She was noted for her quickness . . . is owned by J. W. Ackerman, who has no reason to believe but what he will have the benefit of her services for many years to come . . . .[35]

Ackerman changed the *Dashing Wave's* hailing port to Tacoma, and she is recorded as being of that port in 1886.[36] *The Chronicle*, January 7, 1885, reported that the *Dashing Wave* had gone ashore at Tacoma but was floated off. With some degree of smug, civic pride, the article continued:

> . . . the over 30-year-old ship suffered little harm by her rough experience. The quality of the material and work put into

Piscataqua-built ships in former days is attested by the number of them still afloat and doing good service after thirty or forty years of existence.[37]

In July, 1885, *The Chronicle* again published praise for Piscataqua vessels, quoting from a letter written by Charles W. Walker, former proprietor of the Market House in Portsmouth, which was often the scene of post-launching banquets in the heyday of the clippers. Walker had left Portsmouth and was engaged in the lumbering business in Tacoma, and he "mentioned some of the Portsmouth-built ships of long ago which are still doing good service on the Pacific coast. One of these is the ship (now a barque) *Samoset*, 633 tons register, built on Badger's Island by Fernald & Petigrew in 1847. Another is the ship *Dashing Wave*, 1054 tons, built on the same blocks in 1853. The *Dashing Wave* is slightly hogged [sagging in the middle] but about as fast a sailer as ever, and noted for her quick passages. Both the vesels named are owned by the sawmill company in Tacoma, Wash. Terr., and bid fair for many years of good service yet, if rocks do not get in their way ...."

For those who love good yarns about the Piscataqua's square-rigged ships, more material is available on the *Dashing Wave*, thanks to a devoted researcher named Harold Huyche, then of Edmonds, Washington. Huyche has made some of the details of the *Dashing Wave's* lumbering days available. He found most of his data in *The Weekly Ledger* of Tacoma. Though they seem like odds and ends, they do tell the story of a gallant old lady whose glamorous youth was only a memory, but who was still trying to make an honest living. In a single year the Tacoma mills, where the *Dashing Wave* so often loaded, sent thirty million feet of timber to the Fiji Islands, Australia, New Zealand, China, Chile and Peru. Naturally, the *Dashing Wave* carried only part of that tremendous production. There is in existence a taped interview with a woman whose father, Captain Richard Lancaster, commanded the *Dashing Wave* in her lumbering years. In her girlhood, Irene Lancaster, and the rest of her family, often sailed on the *Dashing Wave*, one of the runs being to Honolulu. She told the interviewers she was "about six" when her father took command, and that was in 1897. Shortly thereafter came the Klondike Gold Rush, and the *Dashing Wave's* owners shipped lumber north to meet the demand for housing. Part of her reminiscence follows:

> You know he [Captain Lancaster] lashed the rudder and backed his sail — foresail — and she went right astern like a steamer. Instead of tacking that's the way he did it across the straits. You could handle her like a yacht. Oh, he loved her. His heart and soul was in her. When he left her it took years off him. If

Dashing Wave *under sail off San Francisco, circa 1900.*
*The Mariners Museum collection.*

    anyone marred the woodwork on her it was like they drove a knife in him. She had a beautiful cabin. It was all white and it had an aqua blue — just a narrow strip that went between the fancy mouldings. Then the gilt. Oh, she was beautiful ... and her dining room — we had an oblong table and the seats were made with a back that you could go back and put them up against the table with your back to the table so you could switch this way to eat. And the mizzen mast went right through the table.[38]

    Captain Lancaster was one of the last commanders of the *Dashing Wave*. The tough old girl was wearing out, particularly in her masts, spars and rigging:

Dashing Wave *as she appeared in final days when stripped down as a barge. National Maritime Museum, San Francisco, collection.*

*Dashing Wave* was sold in 1900 to Thomas Scott and J. A. Stewart of Tacoma ... For two more years she carried lumber under charter to the Tacoma Mill. But like other wooden, square-rigged sailing ships, her days were fast drawing to a close. The *Wave* was worn out aloft as well as below and not worth repairing. During the spring of 1902, she made her final voyage from San Francisco. On March 7, 1902, she was sold to the Taku Canning Co. for the measly sum of $6,000. Then following delivery to her new owners, the old racehorse was ignominiously chopped down to lower masts and converted into a utility barge.[39]

The photograph in this work, purporting to show the *Dashing Wave* under sail in 1910 does raise questions in light of the above paragraph. If the above is correct, then the latest that photo could have been taken would be 1902, and it might have been made when she left San Francisco for the last time. Just how badly worn, below decks, *Dashing Wave* really was is hard to say because eighteen years after being converted to a barge, on March 1, 1920, the *Wave* was in drydock, and close examination showed that her hull was still in first class condition, an expressive tribute to the men who had built her sixty-seven years before. Two weeks after that inspection, loaded with 1,200 tons of materials for the cannery at Taku, Alaska, she stranded on flats in Seymour Narrows, becoming a total loss.

If any vessel ever deserved a eulogy, it would be the *Dashing Wave*, who always gave her owners a full measure of service.

## *Express*

> SPECIFICATIONS: *Packet-type clipper. Tonnage, 1,050. Length, 183 feet; breadth, 35.5 feet; depth, 21.5 feet. Owners, F&P, one-quarter; Peter Marcy, one-quarter; Daniel Marcy, Richard Jenness, Washington Williams and S. C. Thwing, one-eighth each.*

NOT DESTINED for the round-the-world voyages so often the lot of Piscataqua clippers, the *Express*, nevertheless, earned a place for herself in Piscataqua maritime history in two ways, the first being that she was one of the few clippers that left Portsmouth Harbor fully loaded, and the second because of her part in the Civil War. As has been previously remarked, it was the practice to take these ships to Boston under tow, because of lack of out-going cargoes and the impossibility of finding enough Piscataqua seamen to man their rapidly increasing numbers. However, with the *Express* it was different, perhaps because she was locally owned — and her cargo was unusual.

Her launching was on January 28, 1854, at a time earlier than the hour appointed because a steadily rising northwest wind was howling down the river from Great Bay.[40] The *Express* was masted and rigged on the stocks, and after launching, she was taken to Pray's Wharf (in the vicinity of the Granite State Minerals' Pier) and loaded with ice for New Orleans. A keen entrepreneur in Boston had long been promoting the idea of selling ice in southern ports, thus producing cargoes for vessels that would otherwise sail south in ballast. *The Chronicle* made special note that the *Express* was the first clipper loaded by a Piscataqua River firm, the Portsmouth and South Berwick Ice Company. The ice was cut in South Berwick, and brought down river in gundalows. Captain Thomas M. Weeks took the *Express* to sea on February 20, but it was not an easy passage to New Orleans. After leaving Portsmouth, she started leaking at a rapid rate, and upon reaching Montauk Point, the wind blowing strongly from the west, she headed toward New York, where she could be repaired. During the night she went ashore on Hart's Island, but suffered no severe damage. The *Express* was towed to New York, through the twisting, island-dotted channel to the East River. Her leaks plugged, she left New York on March 13 for New Orleans, arriving there on April 3, where her cargo of South Berwick ice was warmly welcomed by those who enjoyed a cool beverage. She was immediately put into the business for which she was intended — transatlantic freighting, principally of cotton. Back and forth she went, between New Orleans and Liverpool. The *Express* did make one passage to the Far East. In May, 1856, she was loaded at New Orleans for Calcutta, sailed on June 28, arriving November 20, a run of 145 days, which was unimpressive. Her return from Calcutta to Boston was not impressive either. In September, 1861, the *Express* was at Eastport, Maine, though it is not clear exactly why.

The outbreak of the Civil War slowed shipping drastically, all the more after the Confederate raiders began harassing U. S. vessels. It was because the *Express* was captured and burned by the *CSS Alabama* that she earned her second niche in the history books. First notice in Portsmouth of the loss of the *Express*, under Captain Charles Frost, was published on October 6, 1863:

> The pirate *Alabama* has destroyed the ship *Express*, Capt. Frost, from Callao, 25 April for Antwerp; *Express* was A-one, 1073 tons .... Capt. Frost has arrived in London.[41]

Four days later, a lengthy letter from Captain Frost was published. It is a first-person account of what happened when the captain of a Yankee ship had the misfortune to fall prey to Captain Raphael Semmes and his British-built *Alabama*,[42] which was manned primarily by Englishmen, and not Confederate sailors. But first to set the stage: the *Express* had been at the Chincha Islands, and there loaded 1,800 tons of guano intended for a Dutch firm in Antwerp. Before leaving Callao, Captain Frost took the precaution of getting the French consul in Lima to certify that the cargo was destined for a neutral power, and only the ship's ownership was American. After passing Cape Horn, the *Express* was in latitude 29° south, 30° 40' west [southeast of Rio de Janeiro] when, in the morning of July 6, a cannon shot was heard. A few minutes later there was a second, and finally a third, this time using shot. Frost made the assumption that it was a distress signal. Despite the foggy weather, he went looking for the stricken vessel. Soon he sighted a steamer, lying hove to, without colors flying. Captain Frost's narrative continued:

> The *Express* was soon boarded by an officer and boat's crew, armed with cutlasses and revolvers. The boarding officer was the Master's Mate, who said he was an Englishman, and hailed from London. He declared the *Express* a prize to the Confederate States *Alabama*, and took possession of her, and ran her in under the stern of the steamer. I was ordered to take my papers to the *Alabama*, where I found, in the captain's cabin, Capt. Semmes, who looked over the ship's papers. I directed his attention to the certificate of the French consul on the back of the bill of lading, declaring, under French seal, the cargo to be neutral property. He replied, "it's only a mere word," and turning to his first lieutenant, he said, "Mr. Kell, we will burn this ship."

> I told him it was certainly neutral property, and requested to have my declaration on oath to that effect, which oath was recorded by the clerk in a book. An offer by me to sign an indemnity bond if he would release her was declined, and I received the impression that everything bearing the American flag was to be burned. I was then ordered back to my ship, and to bring my wife on board the *Alabama*. I was permitted to take a portion of my clothing, but all was taken from me on board the *Alabama*, and what I had on and a portion of Mrs. Frost's clothing was taken also. The officers and crew were allowed one bag of clothing each —They were taken to the *Alabama* and put in irons on the deck in which condition they were kept day and night while I was on board. The ship's papers, log, letters to the consignees, and a private mail from the ship *Shackamaxon*, were burnt. We were on board the *Alabama* 16 days, when we were put on board the ship *Star of Erin*.

Captain Frost's letter ended at that point, but controversy continued. In the same column with Frost's letter, *The Chronicle* reported:

> *The New York Tribune* has a letter, dated Cape Town, Cape of Good Hope, Aug. 19, which makes the following statement—
> "The *Express* carried, besides her Northern register, a Southern one, signed by Jeff. Davis—one of her owners belonging in New Orleans. Captain Frost showed the document to Captain Semmes, and he flew into a passion, and said—'Damn you, I'll burn your ship. You are a traitor, and if it was not for your wife on board I would shoot you.'"

Some months later, in public print, Captain Frost categorically denied that he had ever taken an oath of loyalty to the Confederate States of America. However, the fact remains that Peter Marcy, one of the owners, did live and do business in New Orleans. What could have been more natural than for Marcy to provide a southern registry for a vessel in which he held a quarter interest? Nor would Frost have been required to take an oath of loyalty to the CSA just to carry the document among the ship's papers. Further, in mild defense of Captain Raphael Semmes, the fact his captives were put in irons was really pragmatic from his point of view. If the Yankee seamen had been allowed freedom of the ship, it was almost certain that eventually, as their numbers increased, they would try to capture the *Alabama*. It was the fact that he had more prisoners than he could handle that induced him to release the *Emily Farnum*.

Twelve years and nine months after the *Express* was burned, her owners were awarded damages for their loss by the Commission on *Alabama* claims. A special tribunal, meeting in Geneva, found that Great

Britain's support of the Confederate cause in providing some of the raiders like the *Alabama* justified an assessment of $15.5 million in damages to the United States. The *Alabama* alone destroyed seventy American vessels. "Dreading this elusive raider, Northern shipowners either laid their vessels up, or transferred them to foreign flags. In four years, 1861-64, 750 ships, representing a total of 481,332 tons, were transferred."[43] This wholesale dismemberment of the U. S. merchant fleet was an injury that was long in healing.

After Great Britain yielded to the findings of the international tribunal, Congress established a special commission to receive the claims of all those who had suffered losses at the hands of the *Alabama* and her sisters. Among the Fernald & Petigrew papers, Gertrude Pickett found a statement of the award to Mary E. Petigrew for her husband's one-eighth interest in the *Express*. The basic claim allowed was $5,186.20, to which was added interest from July 6, 1863 to May 1, 1876, a total of $7,845.57. From this sum was taken the commissions of the agents who represented her. Her total award, remitted through Daniel Marcy, was $6,707.96.[44]

## *Midnight*

SPECIFICATIONS: *Half-clipper. Tonnage, 962. Length, 175 feet; breadth, 36 feet; depth, 21 feet. Owner, Harry Hastings of Boston.*

WHEN FERNALD AND PETIGREW first presented their proposal for the construction of the *Midnight*, their intention was to build her entirely of New Hampshire white oak, an unusual plan.[45] However, before signing the final agreement, Henry Hastings stipulated, and Fernald and Petigrew agreed, that the keel be of rock maple, the usual wood for that vitally important part of a ship. But oak was used quite generously elsewhere in the *Midnight*, which had a price tag of $40,000.[46]

It was intended to launch the *Midnight* on April 17, 1854, but stormy weather delayed the ceremony until the next day. She was masted and coppered before sliding down the ways, and, in its account of the launching, *The Chronicle* said, "A new feature in the painting of *Midnight* we noticed. In the cabin the centerpiece of each panel is a landscape or picture of some sort, beautifully done in gay colors—adding much to the appearance of this splendid parlor." The ship's painters were Benjamin B. Swasey and Samuel Rowell, but who did the pictorial art work for them is not known. The *Midnight*'s figurehead was carved by William B. Gleason of Boston, and represented a lion's head, for which Gleason charged $85, plus $25 for bronzing. Gleason's total bill, "which included the carving of the stern moulding, centre ornament, and fourteen letters for the stern, was $271.40.[47] Fifty-four years later, on May 12, 1911, *The Portsmouth Herald*, in an article of reminiscence, said that Edmund M. Brown, whose partner was Samuel P. Treadwell, did the cabinet work. It was said Hastings went $10,000 over the going price to get what he wanted, which was described as being "like a belle in a blaze of glory among the stars of the festive mall."

The traditional post-launching banquet was held at the Franklin House, Congress Street, with Hastings as host.[48] The *Midnight*'s captain was James B. Hatch, who had commanded another of Hastings's vessels, the bark *Kate Hastings*. Captain Hatch took the *Midnight* to Boston, under tow by the *R. B. Forbes*, there to load for the East Indies. Several Portsmouth men went along as passengers on the overnight run: Horatio Coffin, Daniel Marcy, William R. Preston, J. Warren Towle, Leonard Cotton and Samuel Gray. The *Midnight* cleared Boston on June 30, 1854, heading for Calcutta, via San Francisco. Her passage took 117 days, which was the best of her five runs to the Golden Gate. *The Chronicle* reported:

Midnight *on stormy seas. Peabody Museum of Salem collection.*

By recent news from California, we notice the arrival of this ship at San Francisco from Boston, 30 June, and of her sailing for Calcutta, 6 November. On her outward passage she beat all the ships sailing about the same time: *Grace Darling*, *Climax* from New York, 126 days; and *John Land*, sailed the day after *Midnight*, and not yet arrived.

The ships thus beaten by one unassuming half-clipper were first class clippers, built in the vicinity of Boston.

On another occasion, *The Chronicle* reported a race between the *Midnight* and the *Wild Rover* from Calcutta to Boston: "They sailed from Calcutta, March 1, passed the Sand Heads, March 4, *Wild Rover* a full clipper and 300 tons larger, but *Midnight* won."

Through her service, the *Midnight* spent most of her time on the Boston-Calcutta run, earning the Hastings organization substantial profits. But finally her days ran out. *The Portsmouth Weekly* reported on January 26, 1878, that the *Midnight*, under Captain George W. Tucker

Midnight, *painted in China. Peabody Museum of Salem collection.*

of Portsmouth, had been abandoned in the Banda Sea, and commented that the *Midnight* had been thoroughly overhauled only a few weeks before; she was insured for $25,000. Three weeks later the abandonment report was corrected by saying she had put into Amboina, Java, in a leaking condition. She discharged her cargo of petroleum, was condemned and sold for £540. Captain Tucker chartered the bark *Obed Baxter*, also of Boston, to load the *Midnight*'s cargo and carry it to Yokahama, Japan. The *Obed Baxter* had been built two years before in Newburyport, Massachusetts.

## *Noonday*

SPECIFICATIONS: *Medium clipper. Tonnage, 1,189. Length, 200 feet; breadth, 38.5 feet; depth, 23.5 feet. Owner, Henry Hastings.*

TO THE *NOONDAY* goes the distinction of being the last clipper built by Fernald & Petigrew. Before she was launched, Frederick W. Fernald died on April 30, 1855, following his great rival, George Raynes, in death by eighteen days. To the *Noonday* also goes the dubious honor of having a jagged rock named for her. The procedure in the construction of the *Noonday* was much the same as for the *Midnight*, and she was considered a sister ship, although larger. Fernald and Petigrew proposed to Henry Hastings that they build such a vessel, and put a price of $40,000 on it. Hastings accepted.

Gertrude Pickett told the charming little story, without giving its source, of how Henry Hastings personally "went into the woods at West Townsend, Massachusetts, and supervised a crew of workmen in the hewing of white oak timber for his ship. He then accompanied this precious timber as it traveled by rail, wagon and gundalow to its destination ...."[49] That is at variance with a report in *The Chronicle* which declared the white oak to be of the New Hampshire variety, but then *The Chronicle* was ever a promoter of the Granite State. Besides, who could tell the difference between a piece of white oak hewn on the New Hampshire border in West Townsend, Massachusetts, or one cut in the abutting New Hampshire town of Mason? One further consideration gives pause: if that timber was cut and used as suggested, a lot of green timber went into the *Noonday*. Ownership of the *Noonday* was split several ways, with Hastings, the operating owner, holding a quarter interest; Walter Hastings had one-quarter; the Fernald estate, one-eighth; Petigrew an eighth; G. W. Messenger, an eighth; and her captain, William B. Gerry of Marblehead, Massachusetts, the remaining eighth. Gerry had formerly commanded the ship *Cahoota*.

In all probability the death of Fernald slowed the work on the *Noonday*.[50] The impression that Fernald was the guiding genius of the partnership is clear, with Petigrew functioning as an able executive officer. The passing of Fernald also delayed completion of a non-clipper, the *Isaac Boardman*, which was the last vessel built under the aegis of Fernald & Petigrew. In August, 1855, the Fernald and Petigrew yard was bought by John Yeaton, William P. Jones and John E. Salter, but that syndicate did not build any clippers. By that time the clipper fad had almost run its course.

The *Noonday*'s launching was on a Saturday, with the usual gala crowd on hand. It has to be supposed that Henry Hastings, as he had with *Midnight*, entertained his friends at the banquet, with the flow of toasts. However, the *Noonday* did not leave for another month, which provided plenty of time for a young son of John R. Woodman, a carpenter living on Gates Street, to fall off the ship, breaking a wrist and suffering internal injuries. The *R. B. Forbes* took the *Noonday* to Boston on September 24, to be loaded for Calcutta, by way of San Francisco — the run that the *Midnight* was also working. The *Noonday* made four complete passages to San Francisco, the longest being 139 days, which included being stalled around Cape Horn for two weeks. Her best time to the Golden Gate was 117 days, under a Captain Brock, which tied her with her smaller sister. On that second voyage, the *Noonday*, on her way home through the Banda Sea, had problems after striking a rock. When she put into Batavia for repairs, it was discovered she had lost fifty feet of keel, and her bottom was holed. In 1860 she went into the guano trade, loading at the Chincha Islands for Hampton Roads.

On her last passage to San Francisco, she was 139 days out of Boston, on January 1, 1863, as she approached her destination. One version has it that precisely at noon, the *Noonday* struck the rock which became her namesake. The *Marysville Daily Appeal*, however, gave the fatal hour as 2:00 p.m., saying:

> The clipper ship *Noonday* .... struck a sunken rock eight miles from the Farrallones, at 2 P.M. yesterday, and sank in 40 fathoms of water within an hour. All hands escaped in boats. Her cargo was valued at $600,000 .... Steamer *Active* sailed today for the spot where the *Noonday* sank, with the intention of grappling to find her and attaching hawsers. If successful, there will be a slight chance of saving a portion of her cargo.

The *Mercantile Gazette*, in San Francisco, said on January 9:

> ... She struck a sunken rock about a quarter of 12 and sunk at 3 P.M. When she crashed the rock she had all sails set. The weather was clear and the sea smooth, but a heavy swell from the northeast prevailed. After striking the ship swung off and in a very short time sank to her upper deck. The captain, discovering a pilot boat, had turned her landwise with a view to beaching her, but she sank so rapidly that the officers and crew, 24 in number, were forced to take to the boats. They left the ship at 20 minutes to three, and at three o'clock nothing was to be seen of *Noonday* but the American ensign. The pilot boat *Relief* picked up the officers and crew ....

*Angelo Alioti holding the* Noonday *bell, recovered from the ocean in 1934. National Maritime Museum, San Francisco, collection.*

Port officials did not let the *Noonday*'s loss pass unnoticed. A schooner, the *William L. Marcy*, was sent out to locate the shoal where the *Noonday* had met disaster. Returning, the *Marcy* said Captain Henry's bearings were correct, and the newly discovered hazard would be reported to the Bureau of Navigation in Washington. Unfortunately, no action was taken, so the *Noonday* was not the last to be lost on Noonday Rock. In 1873 the *Patrician* piled up on it, and was lost. That did spur Congress to take positive steps about the hazard. With the *Noonday* a complete wreck, it would be expected that the last had been heard from her. But not so! At least one small, but important, part of her has come back from the depths. In 1934, a newspaper reported:

> The disaster of the sinking of the "Noon Day" was recalled yesterday in an extraordinary fashion when Capt. John Tarantino, master of the fishing trawler "Junta" came into Pier 45—with the ship's bell of the Noon Day. After the crew of the "Junta" drew in their nets as they were fishing north of the Farallones, they found in one of them the bell which had been at the bottom of the ocean for nearly three-quarters of a century.

With his brilliant young partner gone, William Petigrew soon associated himself with Daniel Marcy in the building of several vessels at various yards. The former Fernald yard, at the foot of Pickering Street, later became their base of operations.

# IV  *Tobey & Littlefield*

THE THIRD OF THE GREAT Piscataqua clipper-building firms—Tobey & Littlefield—was unique because it endured longer than any of the others, spanning thirty years, and because a company established by one of the partners, Daniel Littlefield, still flourishes in the City of Portsmouth, where change is more the rule than the exception. Littlefield Lumber Company is doing business at 299 Vaughan, across the North Mill Pond from Noble's Island, where Tobey & Littlefield built and launched many fine vessels. The present generation of Littlefields, with reason, takes more pride in the lumber company than in being descended from the famed clipper builder. As one of them put it: "The Littlefields landed in Maine back in 1600 and froze-to-death. There were eleven brothers, and no television, so they have kind of multiplied." Daniel Littlefield came to Portsmouth from Kennebunk, Maine, where he was born on February 22, 1822, and died at the age of seventy-nine. His obituary reads:

> ... He came to this city early in the fifties and formed a co-partnership with Stephen Tobey, and carried on the shipbuilding business on Noble's Island, building some of the best ships constructed on the Piscataqua River, the partnership being kept up for nearly 30 years.
> After the shipbuilding business ceased to be one of the industries of the city, Mr. Littlefield engaged in the wood and coal business, which he carried on right to the time of his death.
> In politics he was a staunch Democrat and represented his party from Ward 1 on the Board of Assessors and as an overseer of the poor.[1]

For years, Daniel Littlefield lived on Russell Street, within a few hundred yards of the shipyard on Noble's Island. Toward the end of his life, he lived on Deer Street, close enough to be active in the daily round of his business. Since his day, fire has twice swept Littlefield Lumber Company, but each time the company has come back strongly, in the tradition that Daniel Littlefield established.

His partner for so many years, Stephen Tobey, was one of those self-effacing men, content to carry on his trade, and getting satisfaction from the merits of his work. Early in the nineteenth century there were several Tobeys — a Stephen among them — building vessels in various yards at the head of the Piscataqua River. In fact, a James Tobey became a partner with Charles Raynes after the latter's break with Frederick W. Fernald, and they built, among other vessels, the *America*, 1,147 tons, for the Kingslands of New York. It could even be that Stephen Tobey's father was the Samuel Tobey who was listed in 1813 as one of the owners of the little schooner, the *Eliza*, built by Joseph Hammond in Eliot.

As a boy, Stephen Tobey was apprenticed to George Raynes, and, when he became a journeyman he continued to work there until he became foreman, a post he held until 1853. At that time, following the great American tradition of free enterprise, he launched himself as a builder, in partnership with Littlefield. It was a logical step because, by that time, it was obvious that George Raynes intended to make George, Jr., his partner, not someone from the outside. In 1886, Tobey, then retired, was described as "the oldest shipbuilder of Portsmouth, who is now living at his nice place in the West End."[2] Tobey had lived for some time next door to his former master, George Raynes. Tobey was the father of three daughters, and he was living with one of them, Martha J. Martin, at the time of his death, on December 6, 1892. His estate of $17,000 was not huge, but was adequate in those uninflated days.

Tobey & Littlefield built their last square-rigger in 1873—the *Grandee*. Others they built in the 1860s included the sister ships, the *Simla* and the *Santee*. Although they built many vessels, they constructed only three clippers. One of them, the *Sierra Nevada*, was the largest launched on the Piscataqua's turbulent waters. It's notable that the firm was versatile enough to build the first merchant steamer on the river, the *General Grant*, in 1863. While the *General Grant* was still on the building ways, a man from Salem, Massachusetts, visited the Tobey & Littlefield Shipyard and wrote a long letter praising the yard highly, saying "the right men are in the right place."[3] The story of those latter-day Tobey & Littlefield ships must wait to be told.

## Morning Light

SPECIFICATIONS: *Full Clipper. Tonnage, 1,713. Length, 220 feet; breadth, 43 feet; depth, 27 feet. Owner, Glidden & Williams, Boston.*

**W**HEN THE *MORNING LIGHT*'S stern hit the waters of the Piscataqua, she was the largest merchant vessel yet launched on the river. Before long she would be surpassed, but not by many tons. If nothing else, the *Morning Light* testified to the complete self-confidence of the new firm. Tobey and Littlefield started out with the biggest vessel yet launched. *The Chronicle* was almost lyrical in its news column of August 27, 1853:

> There is some stir in the new shipyard of Messers. Tobey & Littlefield, on Noble's Island. This once quiet retreat of wooers, lovers, swimmers and anglers, has yielded to the advance of the other "arts;" the broad axe is being plied to the handy oak timber that now strews the once grass-covered ground, and a beautiful ship, the first ever built on the island, has already raised its over-looking prow, that shall ere long cleave a patch around the world. She should be called "Noble."

*The Chronicle* had also burst into poetic eloquence when it reported on the launching, held on Saturday, August 20, 1853:

> The announcement of the launching of the clipper ship *Morning Light*, drew together a large number of people, on Saturday afternoon, to see a common but always interesting occurrence. A larger company than usual were attracted as the ship to be launched from a new yard, by a new firm — this being the first vessel built by Tobey & Littlefield. The last plank that bound her to earth was sawed off about 2 o'clock, & the monstrous ship glided lightly and smoothly into the water, untrammeled by ropes and cables to check her free progress. Everyone pronounced it the most splendid launching they ever saw — a verdict that has been rendered at every launching within the memory of the oldest inhabitant ...

From whom did Tobey & Littlefield get the plans and model to create a river giant? No one knows. It is quite possible that Glidden & Williams, the owners, knew enough about Tobey to provide him with plans prepared in Boston. But that has to be speculation. In every aspect, the *Morning Light* was a daring gamble, and one that paid off.

The *Morning Light* spent only a week on the tidal Piscataqua before she, too, was taken in tow by the *R. B. Forbes*, for the run to

Morning Light. *Painting by Wm. Yorke.*

Boston, never to return. Like all the other Piscataqua clippers, the *Morning Light* attracted much attention in Boston. *The Daily Evening Telegraph* said, on September 21:

> This fine clipper ship has attracted much notice since she has laid at her berth at Lewis' Wharf, and all who have visited her speak in the highest terms of her model and superior workmanship.... Her frame is of white oak, and her planking yellow pine. She is strongly bolted with copper and iron, and in this point inferior to no ship of her size of load.
>
> Her bow is ornamented with a full figure, representing an archer with his bow and quiver full of arrows. The stem is oval, and is ornamented with a gilded chariot, in which is seated the goddess of day, over which is an arch of carved and gilded work. Outside she's painted black.
>
> She has a half poop deck, with a cabin built into it. She has two cabins, the after one is furnished and finished in superior style and ornamented with gilded work. The forward one is also well arranged and painted and grained, and abaft the foremast she has a large house for the accommodation of her crew, galley, store-room, etc. She has a topgallant forecastle, on which there is a large capstan. She is well seasoned with salt, well ventilated with Emerson ventilator, also ventilators along the lines of her plank sheer....

Duncan McLean, writing in *The Boston Atlas*, said:

> ... She has a noble set of spars, and looks like a first-class frigate afloat, her fore and main masts are built and hooped over; the mizzen mast is of a single spar. She has the best of rigging, and was rigged in the best style by Messers Francis Lowe & Co. [A Boston firm].... The ship was decorated by Mr. J. W. Mason, our greatest marine artist, and her blocks were made by Mr. Thos. Shelton, both of this city.

With Captain E. D. Knight, lately of the ship *Queen of the Seas* in command, the *Morning Light* sailed from Boston, October 3, 1853, but had little or no luck with the weather. Her time to San Francisco was 131 days, but her second passage out to the Golden Gate was quite a bit better, and actually her best in five runs. Her captain claimed 112 days. In her fifth passage she was so roughed up that she lost her figurehead. The *Morning Light*'s last voyage under the American flag began in Cardiff, Wales, in August, 1861. Her usual foul luck with the weather hung her up at Cape Horn, but her run from Valparaiso to San Francisco of thirty-seven days was only one short of the record. If it's accepted that she was becalmed right outside Valparaiso for three days, her time would be lowered to thirty-four days, the fastest in history.

The *Morning Light* left San Francisco to load guano at Callao. From there she went to Queenstown [modern-day Cobh], and then to London. The Civil War was then raging, which took some of the edge off profits for American ship owners, and added the hazard of having valuable vessels and their cargoes captured and destroyed. In April, 1863, Glidden & Williams sold the *Morning Light* to James Baines & Co. for service in their Black Ball Line to Australia. Baines paid £9,000 sterling for her, although she had cost Glidden & Williams $117,000, but in those days a pound was worth far more than the current exchange rate. Because the Baines company already had a Canadian-built *Morning Light* in their fleet, the Piscataqua *Morning Light* was renamed *Queen of the South*. What happened to the *Queen of the South* and a lot of other American-built ships after Baines & Company failed in 1866 is not known.[4] She did make a passage from Liverpool to Queensland under the Black Ball in 1864, and in 1865 from London to Queensland. She was sold again on February 1, 1867, and under charter to Melbourne as late as 1869.[5]

Sierra Nevada, *The Mariners Museum collection.*

## Sierra Nevada

SPECIFICATIONS: *Extreme clipper. Tonnage, 1,942. Length, overall, 230 feet; breadth, 44 feet; depth, 26 feet; draft, 23 feet. Owner, Glidden & Williams of Boston.*

THE *SIERRA NEVADA* was the largest merchant sailing vessel launched on the Piscataqua in the nineteenth century. After launching on May 30, 1854, it was reported that "She went off beautifully and sits upon the water like a duck."[6] Before launching, her name was *King of the Forest*, but it was changed, probably at the wish of her owners. Throughout her construction, her commander-to-be, Pearce Wentworth Penhallow of Portsmouth, closely supervised the work. Captain Penhallow took her to Boston on June 6 on the end of a tow line from the *R. B. Forbes*. Such a huge vessel excited a lot of curiosity about the rigging and sail plan that would enable her to move through the water with speed:

> ... She had very square yards, but no flying kites, crossing nothing above the royals. The main yard was 89 feet long; the lower maintopsail yard, 77 feet; upper 70 feet; topgallant yard, 53 feet and royal 42 feet. The yards on the foremast were but slightly smaller: mainmast 91 feet; topmast 52 feet; topgallant, 28; and royal, 18 feet. Bowsprit, 20 feet outboard; jibboom 41 feet; spanker boom, 58 feet, and gaff, 46. She was easy in motion, still and an excellent carrier of sail ....[7]

Apparently she was also a comfortable transport for passengers, sort of a 747 of the sea, because on one passage from London to Rockhampton, Queensland, Australia, in 1870, she carried 497 passengers in the cabins and steerage compartment. Finely finished though she might be, the *Sierra Nevada*'s first assignment was in the smelly guano trade. Captain Penhallow, who held command through her first four voyages, took her from Boston, July 9, 1854, and was ninety-seven days to Callao; loaded at the Chinchas and returned to Hampton Roads on March 16, 1855, and then was ordered to Liverpool. It was on that passage that she began her career of misadventure and records.

On that run she collided with the ship *Janet Leach* of Liverpool, necessitating repairs to her figurehead and bowsprit. For that purpose it was planned to put her into the Wellington Dock at Liverpool. As the mammoth clipper was part way into the dock, needing more than twenty-three feet of water for clearance, she grounded on a mud bank that had accumulated along the sill of the dock. There she hung for more than a week before being eased into the dock for far more serious repairs than originally scheduled. She had broken her back. On the Piscataqua, where she was built, waterfront gossip had it that the tides were ebbing and flooding through her.[8]

Discouraged by the damage reports, the owners put the *Sierra Nevada* up for auction, but the bids did not reach the minimum sought. So she was bid in, and later sold in a private arrangement for $43,750. Glidden & Williams laid their hopes of recovering on their investment by seeking compensation from the dock company. While the repairs were major, they were completed in time for her to be advertised in November as loading for New York. The mishap at Wellington Dock was the subject of bitter litigation for several years because the dock owners, the Mersey Docks and Harbour Board, disavowed all responsibility.

The dragged-out litigation eventually brought about a career change for Captain Penhallow. In the early phases of the case, he continued to command the *Sierra Nevada*, but in 1859 he was commissioned by Glidden & Williams to fight their claims in the British courts. Penhallow was given full powers to serve as the owners' agent. Twice, the dock owners triumphed, but on December 6, 1859, the case went before the Court of Exchequer Pleas at Westminster in London. A complete transcript of the proceedings was published in London in 1860. The trial ended in a victory for the Americans, and was in itself a triumph for English justice.

In essence, the arguments in the case hinged on whether the *Sierra Nevada* was "hogged," or sagging in the middle, when she went into the dock, or whether it had been negligent of the dock owners to have allowed a mud bank to grow around the sill of the dock. The detailed testimony of many persons went into the record. Besides Penhallow, another Portsmouth man, Albert Rand, the ship's carpenter, was a witness. While Penhallow was the plaintiff's agent and man in charge, the American victory was largely the work of James Plaisted Wilde, Q.C., a clever barrister, who became Lord Penzance. Wilde used the defense's own witnesses to destroy the case presented by another able advocate, Sir Fitzroy Kelley, Q.C. In summation, the Lord Chief Baron put the case to the jury in this manner:

> Gentlemen, you have to decide whether you think it really does come down to this — supposing that you do not adopt the theory of Williams [The Mersey River pilot] that the vessel was too late, it comes to this, either there was something that stopped the vessel with reference to the docks — if there was anything what could it be but mud? — or the vessel was actually sagged. It really does come to that alternative ....[9]

The jury came in with a verdict for the plaintifs on December 9, 1859, but before giving it the foreman asked the Lord Chief Baron whether or not the jury would be compensated for the time it had spent:

*The Lord Chief Baron* — Will you give your verdict first, gentlemen?

*The Foreman* — I was told in the room that I was to make that observation first, my lord. Our verdict is for the plaintiff.

*The Lord Chief Baron* — Do you find, in point of fact, that the loss was occasioned by a bank of mud in the dock?

*The Foreman* — We do.

*The Lord Chief Baron* — Do you find that the defendants, by their servants, had the means of knowing the state of the dock, and were negligently ignorant of it, if they were ignorant?

*The Foreman* — We do.[10]

The amount of the damages was not entered into the transcript.[11] Counsel said agreement had already been reached on the point. The plaintiffs also agreed to special remuneration for the jury, which had spent four days listening to a difficult, highly technical presentation.

Insurance firms and ship owners were so impressed with Penhallow's work in the *Sierra Nevada* case that in 1864 he was engaged to represent them on a permanent basis in Liverpool. In March, 1864, Captain Penhallow and his family left Portsmouth for New York, where they took passage in the steamer *City of Manchester*. Penhallow held that post and also worked in the Boston offices of the insurors for many years. He died in Boston on December 6, 1885. Penhallow first went to sea in the ship *Margaret Scott*, 307 tons, built in Durham in 1826 by Joseph Coe. On reaching his majority, he took command of the *Margaret Scott*, later moving to the ship *Rockingham*, and then to other Piscataqua vessels before taking the *Sierra Nevada*. Before he ended his active, sea-going career, he had another scrape with the *Sierra Nevada*: After her return to New York, she was again booked for Liverpool. Early in March, 1856, she went on Romer Shoal below New York, and had to be pulled off. She returned to New York under tow. Penhallow was no longer in command when the *Sierra Nevada* went ashore at Fort Point, near the Golden Gate. She was outward bound for Callao, and, luckily for her, a government steamer was nearby and went to her assistance, "and she was got off immediately, and is lying at Meig's Wharf on the 30th having sustained some damage."[12] Ill-fortune still plagued the big clipper. When she was again ready for sea, having been repaired at the Mare Island Navy Yard for $22,000, she dragged into the clipper ship *Phantom*, suffering another $3,000 worth of damage.

The *Sierra Nevada* made four passages to San Francisco before

Sierra Nevada *renamed as the* Royal Dane *and flying the Union Jack. National Maritime Museum, Greenwich, England, collection.*

1860, and a fifth on the occasion above. It was on her third run, in 1859-1860, that she made the fastest passage to San Francisco of any Piscataqua-built clipper. Captain Penhallow, still in command, claimed ninety-seven days by log, but customs records made it ninety-eight. Also to the *Sierra's* credit is a fast run from Hampton Roads to Liverpool in 1855—fifteen days. Penhallow claimed it as a record.

As was the ending for so many American ships, the Civil War forced sale of the *Sierra Nevada*. In March, 1863, she was sold at London to Mackay & Baines for $52,250. Renamed the *Royal Dane*, she went into the Black Ball Line, England to Australia, and apparently served there until the failure of her owners forced another sale—this time to John Harris. In 1865, the *Sierra Nevada*, seemingly under her original name, was at the Chincha Islands when the *Wild Pigeon*, the George Raynes creation, appeared there as a Spanish government vessel. The *Sierra* was challenged, but sailed out of the Chinchas unmolested.

The *Sierra Nevada* became one of the 151 vessels owned by the Baines and Mackay companies, and was one they were forced to sell in 1866. The *Sierra* apparently had some connection with the Black Ball Line as early as 1861 when she was advertised for Australia, with a bit of boasting about her ninety-seven days to San Francisco. James Baines & Company had an affection for American-built clippers:

> They were bought at bargain prices for the line because of the depressed condition of shipping during the Civil War. Ships like the *Light Brigade, Royal Dane* and the *Young Australia [Red Rover]* proved to be popular and fast on the London to Brisbane run and, indeed, outlasted the Black Ball Line itself.[13]

No matter what her name, the *Sierra Nevada* was ever a challenge in sailing circles. At last, in 1877, the *Sierra* was wrecked on the coast of Chile, en route to Callao for another load of guano. The year she was wrecked, the *Sierra Nevada* was the subject of a hot debate in *The Portsmouth Weekly* as to whether or not she had been the largest merchantman built on the Piscataqua. On September 8, 1877, the paper said the second *Granite State* was rated at 1,689.89 tons, "new measure," and the *Sierra Nevada* was larger. It was the kind of quarrel that delights faddists and students. The *Granite State* was not a clipper, but measured 228.95 feet in length; 41.04 in breadth, 24 feet in depth. The *Sierra's* length, as then given, was 223 feet; beam, 43.5; depth, 26 feet, which would mean "by present measure, 1,672.90 tons, so *Granite State* seems a little larger." Two weeks later a reader wrote:

> I think you are in error in your items relating to the tonnages of the ships *Granite State* and *Sierra Nevada*. *Granite State* does measure 1,693.69, new measure, but I think a careful look at the dimensions of both ships, you will come to the conclusion that *Sierra Nevada* would measure more than *Granite State*. Dimensions are as follows: *Granite State*, 225.95 long; 41.5 wide; 24 feet deep. *Sierra Nevada*, 220.3 long; 43.6 wide; 27.8 deep. *Sierra Nevada*, built by Tobey & Littlefield, was sold foreign before the new measurement was established, therefore, no very close comparison can be made.

The argument was one beloved by all who collect ship specifications as a hobby. The measuring criteria did change with the years, but it is intriguing to wonder what the Mersey Docks and Harbour Board would have made out of giving the *Sierra* a depth of twenty-seven feet. It all seemed to depend on where the measurer first placed his rule. Tobey & Littlefield had one more clipper to put down the ways.

## Ocean Rover

SPECIFICATIONS: *Extreme clipper. Tonnage, 777. Length, 162 feet, breadth, 43 feet; depth, 23 feet. Owners, J. P. Bartlett, Albert R. Hatch, Hill & Carr, Tobey & Littlefield, all of Portsmouth; N. Hanson, South Berwick; McLauren F. Pickering, Greenland.*

**W**HY TOBEY & LITTLEFIELD reduced the dimensions of their last clipper so drastically from those of her predecessors is not known. Speculation would have it that the ownership was entirely home-grown, so to speak, and they might not have wanted to invest the money necessary to rival either the *Morning Light* or the *Sierra Nevada*. As can be readily seen, the *Ocean Rover* was 200 tons less than half the size of the *Sierra*, yet her sharpness still made her extreme in design.

The *Ocean Rover* had one new feature that made her different from the others out of Tobey & Littlefield. A device to facilitate reefing was installed on the *Rover*, one that permitted the operation even in rough weather. Called Foster's patent gear, the apparatus was set up by the riggers after the *Ocean Rover* was launched on September 26, 1854. Frank Miller, editor of *The Chronicle*, wrote on November 16:

> Reefing Topsails — Having never been a sailor, we do not claim the ability to "hand, reef and steer," but on Wednesday we did, without the aid of any person, reef the mizzen topsail of the new ship *Ocean Rover*. To this sail has been attached Foster's Reefing Apparatus, which we have spoken of before. Alongside the wharf it works to perfection, and the riggers say it is just the thing at sea, performing the most difficult operation of reefing topsails speedily and well. The method of operation is this: when the sail is to be reefed, just cast off the haliard and let the yard come down by the run, and the sail is reefed.

Whether Frank Miller was persuaded to try out the device because its inventor, William H. Foster, was running ads in *The Chronicle*, or if it was out of sheer intellectual curiosity is not now possible to know. Equipped with her new reefing gear, the *Ocean Rover*, under Captain McL. F. Pickering, one of her owners, left the Piscataqua on November 29, 1854, to begin her career as a transatlantic packet. She was at Charleston, South Carolina, on December 12, and advertising for cargo for Liverpool. Before leaving Charleston, Captain Pickering made known his great delight in Foster's reefing device, and lauded the inventor in a letter. Pickering said he only regretted that all his topsail yards weren't equipped with the gadget. En route to Charleston, in strong southwest gales, he used it several times.[14] William Foster seized on the letter for its promotional value, and incorporated it in an ad in *The Chronicle*.

Back and forth, the *Ocean Rover* roved the North Atlantic between the southern cotton ports and the busy mills on the Mersey River at Liverpool. In February, 1856, the *Ocean Rover* went on shore near Crosby Point, Liverpool, and early reports had it that her back was broken.[15] However, after her cargo had been unloaded into lighters, a pair of tugs pulled her off, and she was taken into Prince's Dock for repairs.

In 1863, the *Ocean Rover* was bought by a firm in Salem, Massachusetts, for $40,000. It is possible that the *Ocean Rover*'s sale was prompted by an encounter with the *CSS Alabama*. The *Alabama* did meet up with an *Ocean Rover*, described as a bark. Further, in 1884, William H.Y. Hackett of Portsmouth, sitting as an Alabama Claims commissioner, listened to the pleas of the owners of the *Ocean Rover* for damages.[16] Whether the *Ocean Rover*, like so many clippers, had been converted to a bark after her sale is not clear. In 1866, a rigger named Patrick Walsh, formerly of Portsmouth, was killed while rerigging her at Grand Junction Wharf. Walsh fell from the main mast to the deck.

After that, the *Ocean Rover* passed into the ownership of a Captain Carlton. She was lost, July 18, 1870, on a passage from Hamburg to Baker's Island in the Pacific, when she struck a reef in the River Jeganna, Pernambucco, Brazil.

# V  The Hanscoms

FOR MORE THAN TWO CENTURIES, the name Hanscom was synonymous with shipbuilding on the Piscataqua River. The first of the family known to have followed the trade was Thomas Hanscom, who lived in what is now Eliot, Maine, in 1683. He identified himself and his trade on a deed in 1697, signing it "I Thomas Hanscom Shipwright."[1] Then there was a John Hanscom, born in Eliot in 1748, who learned the ship-building trade on what was then known as Castle Island, later Langdon's Island, and is presently Badger's Island.[2] When he was thirty-three, he bought from the Hammond family, also shipwrights of note, the land on which today is situated Green Acre.[3] John Hanscom's sons, William and Samuel, followed their father's trade in partnership for a time, but separated. After the War of 1812 William was apparently associated with Reuben Shapley on Shapley's Island in Portsmouth. From that location he put at least five small vessels in the water, among them the schooner, the *Cossack*, 1814 and the schooner, the *McDonough*, 1815. As his skills and reputation grew, William Hanscom built larger vessels in South Berwick and Durham. Although his major projects seem to have been elsewhere in the Piscataqua valley, Hanscom did establish a shipyard on the family land in Eliot. There in 1828, Master Hanscom, as he was then being called, cut a vessel in two, separated the halves, and built a new middle section, joining them together.

The family's ship-building proclivity extended into the next generation. The oldest son, John, his father's leading apprentice, was lost at sea from one of the vessels he had helped to build. The second son, William L. Hanscom, also worked under Master Hanscom, and showed skill of high order at an early age:

Studying privately, and working for a time in New York, by using the various means for perfecting himself in the business, he thoroughly mastered the theory of naval architecture. He was very successful in teaching the art at Bath; and many of the fine merchant vessels sent out from the City of Ships, owe their good qualities to his masterful instructions.[4]

By 1845, when he was thirty-three, and his father was fifty-two, William L. Hanscom was eager to build ships on his own. He chose the yard in front of Green Acre, where his father had worked, as the site, and in 1847 he built the largest vessel yet launched on the Maine shore of the Piscataqua—the *Elizabeth Hamilton*, 742 tons, which lasted thirty-two years. That was, however, the last major vessel he constructed in the family shipyard. When the gold rush fever claimed him as a victim in 1849, he was building a 135-ton schooner, the *Mary M. Wood*, for Charles A. Wood of Neponset, Massachusetts, and he sailed her to California. History does not relate whether or not Wood and/or his wife went on the passage. Not finding all the gold he had hoped for, Hanscom went to work as a shipwright, commanding the immense wage of $16 a day. He soon gained recognition on the West Coast, and in 1852 he was back in Maine, serving as foreman shipwright at the Portsmouth Navy Yard. From that time on it appears that he worked primarily for the U. S. Navy; he was naval constructor, the top civilian position in those days, in several navy yards. At one point in the 1860s he was actively engaged in trying to recruit shipwrights for three years of service in the Russian navy, but he later returned to federal service. He died in 1881.

It was William's third son, Isaiah, who was the real genius in the family. To him goes credit for the *Nightingale*, the ship that gave the Hanscoms a niche in the halls of maritime immortality. Like his brothers, Isaiah served an apprenticeship under his father; before he was twenty-one he could design and lay down a vessel. In 1845 Isaiah went to work on the Portsmouth Navy Yard. As was customary in those days before Civil Service, political hanky-panky cost him his job when a new president was inaugurated in 1849. Soon he became involved in contracting for various phases of the floating dry dock then under construction for the Portsmouth Navy Yard on Pierce Island. The dry dock was floated over to the Navy Yard when completed. With another shift in the political fortunes of the day, Isaiah was appointed naval constructor at Portsmouth for a period of time. Where did he get his ideas for such radical designs as the *Nightingale?* Possibly from the Pooks, father and son, but Isaiah was right with them.

So, no matter what his achievements for the federal government, Isaiah Hanscom's greatest memorial will always be the *Nightingale*. His dreams were filled with such a vessel, and his designs were put into effect by his uncle, Samuel Hanscom. Samuel was the younger brother William had left behind years ago. Apparently he followed the sea for years before returning to the family interests in Eliot. Being Master William's brother, it is possible that he was associated with William L. Hanscom in the family yard before the latter left for the West Coast. Samuel Hanscom, perhaps aided and abetted by his nephews, turned out two clippers and a square-rigged ship before death overcame him on March 11, 1853. Probate records in Alfred, Maine, indicate that Samuel Hanscom's estate was a tangled mess. Claims against it—those that were allowed—totaled nearly $30,000. William L. Hanscom filed a claim for $16,303, but the administrators allowed him "$00000." Many of the claimants seem to have been workmen in the shipyard itself. As the *Nightingale* story unfolds, it will become apparent why Hanscom was insolvent at the time of his death, but insolvent or not, Samuel Hanscom built one of the most famous, and most notorious, of the Piscataqua and American clippers.

*Nightingale sailing card promoting a voyage to California after her Civil War service. Bostonian Society, Boston, collection.*

## Nightingale

*SPECIFICATIONS: Yacht-like clipper. Tonnage, 1,060. Length, 185 feet on deck; breadth, 36 feet; depth, 20 feet. Owner, Sampson & Tappan.*

CONTROVERSY, SPECULATION, ADMIRATION and deprecation followed the clipper ship *Nightingale* throughout her forty-two years of existence. More words have been written about this sleek, beautifully fabricated Piscataqua clipper than any other launched on the river, and probably more than was written about most of the other clippers launched elsewhere. Isaiah Hanscom's role in her design was not generally known at the time of her building, and speculation over it was rampant. There was even a school of thought that maintained that the brilliant Frederick W. Fernald suggested her lines to Samuel Hanscom, a view which was reinforced by marital ties between the families. But Fernald was busy with the *Typhoon*, and had little time for anything else. That theory could have come from the fact that the design of Typhoon came, at least in part, from plans put together by "young Sam Pook of Boston." Samuel Pook, Sr., who lived at Atkinson and State Streets in Portsmouth, was naval constructor in the 1840s at the Portsmouth Navy Yard when Isaiah Hanscom worked there. It was said that the younger Pook, through his father, made available a model for "a thousand-ton yacht-like clipper."[5] Another delightfully romantic yarn had it that a Swedish count approached Samuel Hanscom and gave him the design of a vessel that would honor Jenny Lind, "The Swedish Nightingale," who was then on a singing tour in the United States under the aegis of P. T. Barnum, the famous nineteenth-century showman.

The *Nightingale*'s keel was laid in January, 1851, and from that time forward she was constantly in the news. From the point of cost, no clipper built on the Piscataqua priced out at more per ton. From the very beginning Samuel Hanscom and his associates were dreaming of making her an exhibition piece at the World's Fair in London, as an example of the ultimate in American ship-building skills. Hanscom obtained financing where he could, and Captain F. A. Miller, who put in some capital, was promised command of the *Sarah Cowles*, which was the *Nightingale*'s original name. Another bit of romance has it that the *Sarah Cowles*'s name was changed after Jenny Lind gave a concert in Eliot for Moses Farmer, the electrical wizard, and some of his friends. It is a fact, however, that Jenny Lind refused to appear on a Portsmouth stage, about the time of the launching.[6] Moreover, it was as the *Sarah Cowles* that the *Nightingale* appeared in early promotional blurbs. In April, 1851, *The Boston Journal* published an ad:

Nightingale, *The Mariners Museum collection.*

### TRANSATLANTIC EXCURSION TO LONDON

The elegant new clipper ship, *Sarah Cowles,* 1100 tons burthen, commanded by Capt. F. A. Miller, now building expressly for the conveyance of passengers on the GRAND TRANS-ATLANTIC EXCURSION TO THE WORLD'S FAIR, landing the same at the port of Southampton, England, will be dispatched from this port about May 20th ....[7]

Despite the optimism of the advertising, all was not going well back on the Piscataqua. Hanscom and Captain Miller were at loggerheads; the financing had bogged down; sub-contractors and workmen were pressing for payment as the over-runs in costs mounted rapidly. One of the problems was that there was no mad rush to book passage, although the clipper's name had been changed to the *Nightingale*. To add to the allure of a luxurious run to England, the builder went overboard in the lavishness of the *Nightingale*'s appointments. An ad was published in Boston, May 7:

### TRANS-ATLANTIC EXCURSION TO THE WORLD'S FAIR

Rare opportunity for a cheap and delightful trip to London. Captain Miller, so favorably known to the public on both sides of the Atlantic as a noble navigator and gentleman, goes out in command of the *Nightingale*. To sail from Boston on or about June 10th. Rate of passage to London and back: first class cabin staterooms, $125. Ladies' cabin, berths, $125; Saloon staterooms, $110. Saloon berths, $100.

However, the *Nightingale* was far from ready to meet the commitment thus advertised. In fact, she was not launched until six days after the sailing suggested in the ad. *The Portsmouth Journal* published a description of her on June 21, 1851, which was so glowing that had it been circulated in Boston it should have drawn patrons:

> The splendid ship *Nightingale*, built especially for the conveyance of passengers to the World's Fair and subsequently to be employed in the China trade, was launched from the yard of Samuel Hanscom Jr., on Monday afternoon. Hundreds viewed *Nightingale's* debut upon our waters, and cheered enthusiastically her first performance. She is built on a real clipper model, having 36-inch dead rise and half floor .... Her frame is all oak, and for strength and beauty of construction she is unsurpassed by any merchant ship built in the United States.[8] As a specimen of American Architecture, she is to proceed direct from Boston to London. Her cabin is to be furnished in an entirely new style, at a cost of $6,000 to accommodate 50 passengers. Her deck will be finished in a superior manner, a pretty and graceful molding being run completely around inside her rail. She has a commodious house on deck for officers and stewards as well as smoking and bathing rooms. Her cordage is from the manufactury of Mr. Jeremiah Johnson of this city.[9] It is made of the best Russian yarn and is pronounced by competent judges fully equal to any that can be obtained from any source. The *Nightingale* was modeled by Mr. Hanscom, her builder, designed by Capt. F. A. Miller, under whose superintendence she has been constructed. Her keel was laid in February and it is intended to have ready to leave here for Boston on the 23rd inst.

Unfortunately, favorable reviews in newspapers seldom dispel financial problems and the tangle seemed insoluble. In an effort to clear up the situation, Ichabod Goodwin of Portsmouth, who was an experienced mariner and businessman, was appointed agent. His management was masterly, and perhaps provided basic training for the time when he would be New Hampshire's first Civil War governor, able to raise three regiments almost on the worth of his word. Also of real assistance to Samuel Hanscom was his son, Justin V. Hanscom, who years later became the trusted right hand of Frank Jones, the Portsmouth ale brewer.[10]

The *Nightingale* was towed to Boston, where she was tied up for six weeks while Goodwin worked out her financial salvation. Davis & Co. bought the *Nightingale* at auction on September 6, for $43,500, and that company, working closely with Goodwin, supposedly straightened everything out. Exactly how it was done is not clear; the figures needed for full understanding simply are not available. However, Goodwin's financial legerdemain was such that "even Hanscom and Miller were paid in full for their work."[11] If that was indeed so, it makes it difficult to understand why Samuel Hanscom was so much in debt when he died two years later, unless he ran into financial problems with the two other ships he built because of poor management.

Still another romantic notion about the *Nightingale* has been scotched by the above facts. For years the story that the ship was built to take the "Swedish Nightingale" back to her homeland has had credence. None of the facts seem to fit this idea, and the advertising quoted above rebuts it. But she was not able to fulfill the purpose for which her construction had been speeded up, which was exhibition at the World's Fair. By the time her finances had been straightened out, it was too late for any trip to London, and the plan was abandoned. Instead, she went immediately into the Australian trade, sailing from Boston on October 18, 1851, under Captain John Fiske. The *Nightingale* was the first American vessel to enter that business. Her total time to Sydney was ninety days, and parts of the passage were quite fast, giving hope for speedier runs in better weather. From Australia, the *Nightingale* went to Whampoa (Canton). On one of her visits to Canton and Shanghai, she met the clipper the *John Wade*, one of whose passengers was an American businessman named George Francis Train. Train wrote:

> I know the ship; it is the clipper launched for the World's Fair, the *Nightingale*. Next to a beautiful woman, give me an American clipper. I like them both, but as I have not yet seen the former in Indian or Asiatic seas, I am more than delighted to find a fellow countryman in the latter, for one sits as proudly on the water as a Western nightingale at her piano.[11]

On her first voyage, the *Nightingale* also disappointed her admirers by taking 133 days from Canton to London. Yet on one leg of the journey she was near the record time. Captain Fiske was so upset with her performance that he left her in London, and the owners had to send over Captain Samuel W. Mather to take command. Fiske later commanded Fernald & Petigrew's *Dashing Wave*. The owners were still so confident in the sailing ability of the *Nightingale* that they offered to put up stakes of $50,000 for a race to China and back. Again, despite romantic ideas to the contrary, there were no takers. Her second voyage was from London to Shanghai and return. Captain Mather was a driver, and stories were told of him leaving on sail when his officers and crew were begging him to reef. On that outward run, she was faster than any others except the American clipper, the *Challenge*. After her return to London, she went to New York, and was loaded for Australia. She sailed May 20, 1854, with freight and 125 passengers; her passage was only seventy-five days. Not until 1859 did she visit San Francisco, taking 148 days because of bad weather all the way. Returning to New York, she began the dark chapter in her life story. The *Nightingale* was attached because her owners were having financial problems. She was then sold to a Salem company, who sent her to Rio de Janeiro, where she was again sold, probably with the full knowledge that the new owners intended to use her as a slave ship. From the time of the first Baltimore clippers, the slave trade had liked sleek, fast vessels for their cruel traffic, and the *Nightingale* had both those qualities, in addition to ample size.

Her new commander was really Francis Bowen, who had a Brazilian posing as captain. Bowen had a substantial investment in the *Nightingale*. Bowen was one of those amoral men who continually tread the borderline between rascality and respectability. The *Nightingale* sailed to England, where Bowen told his crew they were going to Bombay, India, for cargo. In March, 1861, Bowen was cruising the *Nightingale* along the African coast, stopping here and there, making arrangements to pick up a cargo of slaves. Also on the African coast was the *USS Saratoga*, under Captain Alfred Taylor, whose mission was to capture slavers. Slave running, or "blackbirding," as it was once called, was a sensitive political issue because the importation of slaves into the United States had been illegal since 1807. American and British warships habitually cruised in African waters looking for slavers.[13] Slavery was one of the basic causes of the civil war that was on the eve of erupting in the United States. The *Saratoga* and Bowen were well aware of each other, and they played cat-and-mouse for several days. The slippery Bowen eventually managed to load 960 unfortunate blacks, some of whom were already seriously ill and starving from weeks spent in the barracoons, as the African slave pens were called.

Unable to catch Bowen loading his victims, Captain Taylor went through the motions of sailing away from the coast, then slipped back, in the dead of night, and caught Bowen with his shipload of human misery. Captain Taylor put Lieutenant John L. Guthrie on the *Nightingale* as prize master, but 160 of the slaves-to-be died before they could be taken to Liberia and freed. From there Lieutenant Guthrie took the *Nightingale* to New York, first helping Francis Bowen to make his escape — at least,

Bowen later attributed his freedom to Guthrie, who was a southern slave owner. Bowen made his way to Boston, but fled when he discovered there was a reward for his capture, making his way to Havana. A friend once said of Bowen:

> He could be kind and cruel, generous and selfish, logical and utterly irrational, good and bad, all in the same brief hour .... He was the son of a New York merchant, but was the family black sheep ....[14]

In 1866 the men in the *Nightingale*'s crew that had not been sent to New York in her, under the prize master, petitioned the Congress for compensation because they had been detained and so did not participate in the prize money. A House committee saw no need for redress: "the government having landed them in New York and furnished them with new suits of clothing, free of expense."[15]

Arriving in New York without Francis Bowen, the *Nightingale* was condemned on July 2, and sold at auction for $13,000. She was promptly chartered by the U. S. Navy, and immediately put to work hauling coal to the Key West Navy Yard, where she served as store ship for the outpost. The Navy eventually bought her, and four thirty-two pounders were installed in her. Her honorable but unspectacular naval service may have atoned a little for the foul trade in which she had been engaged on the African coast. The *Nightingale* was orderd to Boston, May 17, 1864, because she was thought to be contaminated by yellow fever, which really would not have been a good turn for Boston, if it was true. Fortunately, no epidemic ensued after her arrival. When the Civil War ended, the Navy auctioned her along with many other redundant vessels. She returned to civilian life under the command of Captain David D. Mayo, who loaded her for San Francisco where she arrived, March 9, 1866, 119 days from Boston. Captain Mayo put her up for sale, and the Western Union Telegraph Company bought her for $23,381. At that time the telegraph company was visualizing a cable line across the Bering Strait, then across Siberia and into western Europe. But that came to naught.

The *Nightingale* had various owners and adventures over the next decade, making her last appearance in San Francisco in 1876. At that time she was described as "being so beautiful and dainty as to make a sailor weep for joy."[16] Returning to New York, she was again sold, this time to Norwegian lumber merchants who employed her in that trade in the North Atlantic. Her name was unchanged, and she still had her reputation for making fast passages. It was on a run between Quebec and London that she was abandoned at sea on April 5, 1893, at the ripe old marine age of forty-two. Her crew was taken off by a passing vessel.

The *Nightingale* was long gone by 1939, but she was not forgotten. When World War II began in Europe, the U. S. Maritime Commission started expanding the American merchant fleet. Twenty of a new, C2 class of freighter were built and named for famous clippers. The *Nightingale* was so honored. Built in Newport News, Virginia, the new *Nightingale* underwent many name changes. Turned over to the British in 1941, she became the *Empire Egret*. Back in U. S. registry in 1942, she was renamed the *Santa Isabel*. Then she became the *Guiding Star*, and was later mothballed until 1973. She was scrapped "as of Aug. 6, 1973."[17]

## Josephine

SPECIFICATIONS: *Tonnage, 947. Length, 170 feet; breadth, 33 feet; depth, 23 feet. Owner, Gen. Joseph Andrews, Salem, Mass.*

THE REMEMBERED NOTORIETY of the *Nightingale* casts the *Josephine*, her younger sister, in the role of ugly duckling. *Josephine* did attract some attention in the spring of 1852, but she is not listed in many books by clipper authorities. Be that as it may, *The Portsmouth Journal*, on February 28, 1852, gave good notice of the *Josephine*. Moreover, many of the Piscataqua craftsmen who worked on her were cited:

> Fast as one ship goes another new one appears at one of our wharves; each vieing with the other in claims either to model, strength or beauty.—The above ship *Josephine*, of 947 tons, was built at the yard of Samuel Hanscom, Jr., in Eliot, about three miles above Portsmouth Bridge, for Gen. Joseph Andrews of Salem. She is a well built ship, and although an effort is made to avoid all gaudy appearances, she is truly handsome, and her proportions are so good as to deceive the eye in estimating her size.
>
> She is built of the New Hamsphire white oak, which like the Granite Hills, is famous the world over. She is 170 feet on deck, 36 feet wide, 22 feet 6 inches deep; has two entire decks and a full poop 84 feet long, and a house between the fore and main mast, 34 feet for offices, galley, &c., and a top gallant forecastle for the crew.—The cabin is the largest we recollect having visited, being 45 feet in length. The accommodations for passengers are excellent. The cabin is finished in a rich but not gaudy manner, and furnished in Mr. S. M. Dockum's usual good style. The veneering of the cabin was done by Mr. A. T. Joy [A cabinet maker at 42 Market St.] Portsmouth, and the joiner work by Mr. S. Amos Trott [Penhallow Street]; the painting was done by Mr. L. A. Bruce, Market Street.
>
> The *Josephine* is to be commanded by William Jameson, of Saco, under whose superintendence she was built. She will sail early next week, probably for New Orleans. Success to these children of the Piscataqua.

Early in her career, the *Josephine* was leased to the Empire Line, under Captain Charles Lenholm. Like so many of her contemporaries, with the continuing California boom, the *Josephine* was put into that trade. She left New York on May 25, 1852, taking 147 days to reach her destination, three of them lost at Valparaiso for repairs. On that passage her cargo was consigned to William G. Wendell, a commission merchant, who had his roots in Portsmouth, New Hampshire. Wendell went out to the West Coast with the 1849 Gold Rush, but found his lode in merchandising, and was still there in 1898.

In June, 1859, under Captain William Jameson, the *Josephine* burned in St. Louis Harbor, Mauritius, while on a passage across the Indian Ocean.

The *Josephine* ended the clipper-building efforts of the Hanscoms. However, they did put another square-rigger in the water: the *Judge Shaw*, 700 tons, which was described in a news item as a "half clipper." The *Judge Shaw* was apparently found lacking in clipper qualities, and with that the Hanscom yard went out of business, for all intents and purposes.

# VI  *The Badgers*

**F**OR NEARLY A CENTURY the Badgers helped in creating the legends and traditions of Piscataqua ship-building. Their regime as master shipbuilders started in the late eighteenth century with William Badger, who became known as "Master Badger." A native of Newfields, New Hampshire, he was apprenticed at a young age as a shipwright. It was a trade he followed at various locations in the Piscataqua Basin. The site most commonly associated with his name is present-day Badger's Island, where he lies in a long-neglected tomb. On the island, he worked under the master shipbuilder James Hackett, in John Langdon's shipyard. That was in Revolutionary days, a time when Langdon had been able to wangle contracts for the construction of two frigates for the Continental Navy, the *Raleigh* and the *Ranger.* Later on, Langdon won a contract to build the seventy-four gun ship *America*. In addition, Langdon's yard also turned out the successful privateer *Portsmouth*, and other small vessels. It was 1797 when William Badger took up residence on the island that now bears his name, and became his last resting place. He made it his home for the rest of his life.[1] When the building of war vessels slackened after the Revolutionary War, Badger built some smaller craft in the vicinity of Newmarket. However, the international tensions building up in the late 1790s dictated a boom in naval construction, and brought about Badger's return.

At that time it was confidently expected that the U. S. Navy would acquire Langdon's Island for the first public navy yard, but the $25,000 price tag for eighteen acres scared off Benjamin Stoddert, the first secretary of the navy, and the founder of the Portsmouth Navy Yard. Stoddert's hesitancy proved pragmatic when the government was able to buy Dennett's Island for $5,500. When the building of warships subsided,

*Clipper builder Samuel Badger.*

the Langdon yard became available. William Badger bought the yard and three acres of land that took in the northwestern tip of the island that now bears his name.[2] In 1801 he launched his first merchant vessel from the island, the *Bristol Packet*, a 249-ton ship. For the next twenty-nine years, Badger launched vessels of all models on the Piscataqua.

Other Badgers were closely associated with him. William Jr., joined his father in the shipyard as an apprentice, and was obviously the heir apparent to the Badger Shipyard, but he died on December 31, 1830, less than a year after his father.[3] Master Badger's brother, Robert, worked in the yard, as did a nephew, Samuel, who became a master builder in his own right and constructor of the Badger clippers. Still another Badger, David, worked with Samuel in the latter's yard on Kittery Foreside.

Tradition has it that Master Badger had his 100th vessel on the stocks the day he died, February 22, 1830. However, even an esteemed maritime authority like William E. Dennett of Kittery has been unable to establish that number. A count of William Badger's vessels, listed in the customs records from 1800 until his death, gives only fifty-one. His sadly neglected tomb on Badger's Island has an inscription on it to the effect he produced "nearly one hundred vessels." However, whether the claim is fact or fiction, it cannot be disputed that Master Badger was a prodigious builder of vessels. In its obituary of Master Badger, *The New Hampshire Gazette* said:

> ...Though his years were prolonged beyond the ordinary limits in the life of man, yet his loss will be deeply and sensibly felt by all his surviving relatives. In the death of Mr. Badger, the public also have sustained a loss. He was one of the most extensive shipbuilders in this section of the country. More than one hundred vessels of different classes have been built by him since his establishment in business. It is a tribute due his memory to say that all his business transactions were characterised by the most sterling integrity which justly procured for him an enviable reputation. In his domestic and social relations, he furnished an example worthy of imitation. He was an affectionate husband, an indulgent father, and a faithful friend.[4] He died, as he had lived, a firm believer in the ultimate happiness of the human race. The last words he articulated were "Come, Lord, I am ready."

There are a couple of other versions of Master Badger's final hours. One has it that even as he lay dying, he insisted that he would be coming back to lay another hundred keels. The news item concluded with a note of regret: "But it is not supposed the 'Old Man' would undertake to return to his occupation in times such as these."[5] Still another tale is that

*Samuel Badger tombstone, private cemetery, Kittery, Maine. Bust sculpted by David French. Author's photograph.*

Samuel Badger, his nephew, paid a man to sit "by his revered uncle's bed throughout the night, so as to take notes of anything the delerious shipbuilder might say as concerned the construction of vessels.[6] However, that one seems a bit ridiculous. Samuel had worked so closely with the "Old Man" for so many years there would be few secrets he did not know. Study of Master Badger's will makes it clear why Samuel Badger spent only another year or so in the Badger Shipyard on Badger's Island. Exactly what prompted William Badger to include the following clause can only be speculated upon:

> I give, bequeath and devise unto Samuel E. Coues of Portsmouth, in the County of Rockingham, and State of New Hampshire, Merchant, and Joseph Sherburne, of the same Portsmouth, Husbandman, in trust for my son William Badger, the dwelling house where he now lives, and its appurtenances and the land adjoining the same which he has heretofore occupied and improved, for and during the years of his natural life, subject to this restriction, that they shall not alienate or lease the same for a longer, at any one time, than one year; and also the right and privilege in my shipyard of building or repairing any vessel, *not exceeding one at a time* [Emphasis added.], which my said son William Badger may personally contract to build or repair.[7]

While positive information is lacking, it can be conjectured, largely because the death of William, Jr. followed so soon after the father's, that Master Badger was aware his son might die at an early age. Therefore, he set up the trust, one of the trustees being his son-in-law, Joseph Sherburne. Further, Badger forgave all of his son's debts to him. Nowhere in the will is Samuel Badger, the nephew, given any consideration. The strictures in the will, as to the use of the shipyard, were such that no ambitious man could accept them, and Samuel Badger was both ambitious and industrious, as his subsequent ship-building career established. Before leaving the old yard Samuel Badger finished the ship *Howard*, 399 tons, and built the *Apollo* in 1831, 413 tons; besides being the last, this was also the largest vessel launched by a Badger from Badger's Island. William Badger's shipyard eventually passed out of the family. As related previously, it became the site from which Fernald & Petigrew launched their clippers. Old William Badger, as he specified in his will, is buried "on my land between my orchard and Zebulon Willey's division fence, about thirty or forty feet below my barn..." In 1888, a news item reported that the counting room, "formerly occupied in ship-building times by Raynes & Fernald and Fernald & Petigrew, at Badger's Island, has been occupied the past three years by a private family. The lower part of the island, has been built upon by cottages..."[8]

If Samuel Badger did get secrets of how to build bigger vessels from his bedside eavesdropping, he lost no time in applying them in his new shipyard on Kittery Foreside, approximately where Boulter's coal wharf once stood. Between 1832, when he launched the *Charlotte*, and 1839, when the *Franconia* was finished, he put nine vessels in the water, only two of which were not square-riggers. During the 1840s twelve ships came out of his yard, the largest of which was *Hibernia*, 877 tons. The other major yards, George Raynes and Fernald & Petigrew, in the former Badger yard, were well into the clipper business, along with the Hanscoms, before Samuel Badger built the *Fleetwood* in 1852. Only two more of the square-riggers built by Badger fell into the clipper classification: the *Granite State* (1854) and the *Cathedral* (1855). The latter was rated as a "half-clipper."

Samuel Badger's yard faced directly toward the launching ways of the famed Franklin Shiphouse at the Portsmouth Navy Yard.[9] Here Samuel Badger spent twenty-seven years building vessels. He died in September, 1857, at the age of sixty-three. The inventory of his estate included his house, the shipyard, two acres on the north side of the road leading to the Navy Yard, and some property held in partnership with John Neal, the husband of his daughter, Ann.[10] Samuel and Lois Badger were the parents of six children: Ann, Margaret, Apphia, Samuel

A., Ella E. and James M. Samuel Badger is buried off of Otis Avenue in Kittery, not much more than a cable length from his shipyard. The plot is probably in a corner of the two acres he owned "north of the Navy Yard Road."

Samuel's death did not end operations at the shipyard. His son-in-law, John Neal, continued there, although he did not construct any clippers. He did, however, produce several vessels over the next two decades. One of these ships was the *Portsmouth* (1858), and another was the second *Granite State* (1877), which might possibly have been a bit bigger than the *Sierra Nevada*. The *Granite State* was built for Daniel Marcy. One of the Badger's collateral relatives, David O. Badger, was a shipwright for many years, much of the time working for Daniel Marcy. By 1879, however, David Badger had turned so far from shipbuilding, by then a dying industry, that he was farming in Newington. *The Chronicle* reported on October 22: "He sends daily to our market some of the best vegetables seen in town. His bed of onions is the largest and best raised in Newington." It is possible that he took part in constructing Marcy's *Granite State*, and that probably was the last sailing ship in which a Badger was involved. David O. Badger died fairly young, but his son, Daniel Badger, later became mayor of Portsmouth and put the city's Red Light District out of business in 1912.[11] That, too was a seafaring business of a sort.

A news item published in 1886 served as kind of an obituary for the Badger yard: "The former shipbuiding yard of Master Samuel Badger at Kittery, where so many fine ships were built in years long past, directly opposite the launching ways of the Franklin Shiphouse at the Navy Yard, is being replanted by John Neal, Esq. It produces abundant crops, the soil being rich from the decay of vegetable substances these many years."[12] Among those fine ships were three clippers.

## Fleetwood

SPECIFICATIONS: *Tonnage, 663. Length, 146; breadth, 31 feet. Owners, Sewall, Johnson & Co. of Boston, and Captain Dale.*

TO THE *FLEETWOOD* goes the distinction of being the smallest clipper built on the Piscataqua. A little mystery surrounds her construction. Several authorities, for some unknown reason, credit her to George Raynes, yet there is no doubt she was the product of Samuel Badger's yard. A leading source substantiating this is *The Portsmouth Chronicle*, which reported on August 16, 1852, only two weeks after its own "launching," that "Samuel Badger is building a ship of 600 tons..." That item was followed on October 13, 1852, with:

> Launching. Today at 11 o'clock, from the yard of Samuel Badger, the 600-ton *Fleetwood*, which is for the Calcutta trade, and is owned by Sewall, Johnson & Co. of Boston, and is to be commanded by Capt. Frank Dale of Gloucester.

The *Fleetwood* was rigged on the Piscataqua before being towed to Boston in mid-November by the *R. B. Forbes*. The first of December she cleared for San Francisco, and *The Chronicle* commented:

> This beautiful ship has loaded her entire cargo, in the Davis & Co. line for California, in the short time of five days, and is now full, is completely engaged. She lies at Long Wharf, Boston. Her between decks are finished equal to any cabin. From San Francisco she will proceed to Shanghai for a cargo of tea directly for Boston.

The *Fleetwood*'s first passage to San Francisco took 130 days, fifteen days slower than the best time of the *Tinqua*, which was the larger by only five tons. The *Fleetwood* unloaded in July and went on to Shanghai. After leaving that port for home, she had to put back because of the illness of Captain Dale. She returned to Boston, March 23, 1854, having done a little rescue work on March 20 when she took a crew of six off a sinking schooner. *The Chronicle*, on March 29, quoted *The Boston Transcript*:

> The ship *Fleetwood*, Capt. Frank Dale, that arrived on Thursday from China, came into port in the finest order that we ever saw in a ship entering the Port of Boston. Both outboard and inboard, on deck and aloft, she presented a most beautiful and trim appearance. She brought a full cargo of tea and cassia [Cinnamon].

Next she went to London, returning to Boston on September 13, and then loaded and sailed for Calcutta, being 116 days on her passage. Leaving Calcutta on April 16, 1855, she was 113 days getting to Boston. The *Fleetwood* left Boston on February 12, 1859, on her last voyage. Her destination was Honolulu, but off Cape Horn the little clipper ran into bad weather. She collided with an iceberg at five o'clock in the morning of May 3, 1859, and soon flooded. Well equipped with boats, the mate and four seamen took one, while Captain Dale, his wife and son, a passenger and thirteen seamen took another. The mate and his party were picked up, But Captain Dale's boatload was never heard from again.

## Granite State

*SPECIFICATIONS: Tonnage, 1,108. Length, 174 feet; breadth, 34 feet; depth, 24. Owners, Horton D. Walker, Samuel Billings, J. N. Tarlton, William Simes, J. T. French, George W. Pendexter, Samuel Clark, all of Portsmouth; Samuel Badger, John Neal and J. F. Mathes, all of Kittery.*

T HE *GRANITE STATE* won quick fame of a sort along the Piscataqua for her refusal to get wet. It was planned to launch her before dawn on December 7, 1853, but a snow and sleet storm iced her to the stocks. Workmen finally built fires alongside, and the heat released her at last. She went into the water fully rigged. Under Captain Samuel Billings, one of the owners, she cleared for Mobile early in January, 1854, and entered the cotton trade between southern ports and Mobile and Havre. After several transatlantic runs, she was loaded for Smyrna (Now Izmir, Turkey) in March, 1855, going by the way of Liverpool. In September, 1855, a news item gave some hint of the cruel and abusive treatment sailors often suffered at the hands of bucko mates:

> Before William H. Y. Hackett, U.S. commissioner, Edward McNulty, a seaman on the ship *Granite State*, complained against Samuel Billings, captain, and William Valentine, second mate, for assault and a severe beating. Testimony shows that Valentine on Aug. 27, at sea, cruelly beat and abused McNulty (who was disabled by a lame hand) for not going aloft as ordered in the night by the mate. McNulty ran for refuge or redress to the Captain, who, instead of relieving him, justified the mate.
>
> The commissioner freed the Captain on the ground that he was not fully aware of McNulty's disability, but he held the mate in $200 bail for the U.S. Court on Oct. 2. Four witnesses were bound over in $50 each.[13]

Much of the *Granite State's* career is obscure. Apparently she often cruised to India. In October, 1856, B. F. Farnham of Boston and John H. Sheafe of Portsmouth, a supercargo, came from Calcutta in her, along with a Mrs. Weeks of South Berwick.

The *Portsmouth City Directory* for 1857 lists Captain Nathaniel G. Weeks of Greenland as master of the *Granite State*. Although the fate of the *Granite State* is not known exactly, she was probably lost in 1868.[14]

## Cathedral

SPECIFICATIONS: *Half clipper. Tonnage, 1,650. Owner, Enoch Train Company.*

THE *CATHEDRAL* WAS THE LARGEST VESSEL ever built by Samuel Badger. Unfortunately, no authority seems to have her dimensions other than tonnage, and the 1857 *Portsmouth City Directory* credits her to George Raynes. But the *Cathedral* definitely was built by Badger, with Captain Daniel Marcy as ship superintendent, and her future commander, Captain William H. Howard, was often in attendance.

She was launched, March 3, 1855, a little behind schedule. The occasion was celebrated with a banquet in Josiah G. Hadley's Piscataqua House on Pleasant Street, Portsmouth, where the former federal building, built a year or two later, now stands. The owners sent their tug, the *Enoch Train*, to the Piscataqua to get her. From Boston, the *Cathedral*, described as a packet ship, sailed on April 17 for Liverpool with a large number of passengers, and cargo valued at $260,000. From the fact that she was intended to carry passengers, it can be safely assumed that the *Cathedral* met all the Piscataqua traditions of luxury in cabins and staterooms. Why she was taken off the Liverpool run and sent to Callao can only be speculated, but the transatlantic traffic may have slackened. The voyage ended in Philadelphia. Her next assignment, and last, was a run to San Francisco. Off Cape Horn, she was lost. Her chief officer, A. R. Clarke, filed a report to the Enoch Train Company, which was printed by the *Panama Star & Herald*, and reprinted by *The Chronicle* on May 4, 1857. For its graphic description of shipwreck off Cape Horn, it is worthy of publication:

> Gentlemen:—It is with sincere and heartfelt sorrow that I write to announce to you the total loss of your noble ship *Cathedral*, and her gallant, ill-fated commander, Wm. H. Howard, which took place off Cape Horn, on the afternoon of Wednesday, Feb. 17th, 1857, while in latitude 59° 14′ S, and longitude 69° 38′ W. The full details of this disaster I shall now proceed to detail.
>
> At about 2:40 P.M., while lying to under close-reefed topsails, fore storm sail and full spencer, the ship heading to the southward and westward, wind about N.N.W., a tremendous sea struck the ship, and a heavy squall passing at the same time, she fell immediately over on her beam ends. The captain being unable to leave his berth on account of illness, (he having been very unwell for a week previous, so much so that at one time I gave him up for a dying man.) I proceeded at once to inform him of the situation of the ship, and to request his orders. He directed me to

use every means in my power to right the vessel, and not cut away the masts except as a last resource.

I found, however, that no other means would avail and accordingly gave the order to cut away the mizzen mast, which was done, but without any good effect. The main mast was the next cut away, and, as it went overside, it carried away with it the galleys, upon which were lashed the Captain's gig, the two life boats, and a whale boat. As I then perceived that the ship did not pay off, but lay dead in the trough of the sea, settling more every moment, and as the carpenter reported that water was rushing into the 'tween decks through the forward scuttle, I directed the second officer to go forward and clear away the long boat, which was lashed on the forward side of the forward house, while I went below and informed the captain of what I had done. I told him that in my opinion the Vessel would go down in a very short time, and requested him to allow me to have him carried and placed on board the boat.

This, however, he refused, declaring that he would never leave the ship, and that boat could not live five minutes in such a sea. I then went again on deck, when the third officer informed that the topsides were open, the coal falling out and the water rushing in. I again went below to the captain, to inform him that the ship was rapidly settling, and to beg him to go with me, but he refused, and, as I was endeavoring to prevail upon him, the ship fell over full upon her side, and the water immediately half-filled the cabin. The Captain then cried out to me, "For God's sake save yourself," and, as I perceived that the vessel must go down in a very few minutes, and that no time was to be lost, I broke out the window on the weather side of the cabin, and first pushing out the Doctor (who had remained by the Captain until then) through the window. I followed him myself, and ran along the bilge of the vessel, outside her channels, and leaped down upon the side of the forward house, breaking it through, and falling in up to my shoulders. I immediately got out, and leaping into the water, was picked up and placed in the boat, which had been floated off the house by the sea, so far had the vessel gone down in the water.

Having picked up all whom we could, though, owing to our having no oars, we were obliged to leave the Doctor and one man on the wreck, as they would not jump overboard, and we could not get near them, we shoved off, and had hardly gotten 15 yards from the ship, when a tremendous sea struck her, lifted us up, swept us around her stern, and covered her at once from our sight. We saw nothing of her afterwards, except a few pieces of board and one spare spar.

It was just 40 minutes from the time the ship was thrown on her beam ends until she disappeared from sight.

When the main mast carried the four after boats over the side, all the oars which were on deck being lashed inside of them, of course went also, and the spare oars were below, and of course inaccessible to us.

We found ourselves 36 in number, on board an open boat with neither oars nor sails. One half our number — the watch which was below at the time of the accident being in the clothes they had left their berths in, with nothing but three or four pieces of batten, a piece of the loom of an oar, and a small bit of board which we broke from the bottom ceiling of the boat to keep her head to the wind.

During the whole time of the disaster a bark and a ship were in sight of us to lee ward, the bark, at the time the ship went down, being distant about three miles, bearing about S.E. Towards her all our hopes were directed, but we soon found she drifted to leeward faster than we did, and that our only chance would be to put the boat before the wind, and run down to her. This, after much trouble, we succeeded in doing by making some of the men stand up in the bows of the boat and spread out their oil jackets, and after several hours of hard bailing and keeping the boat before the wind, we rounded under the stern of the bark *Ann Pitcairn Sharp*, of Maryport, England, Capt. Robert Claister Sharp, to whom, under Providence is due our lives. He had hove to on seeing our disaster, determined to wait until daylight, and then run over the spot to see if anyone could be picked up, as neither he nor his officers expected for a moment that any boat could live in such a sea, and owing to the squalls which were constantly passing, it was impossible for him to see us so far to the windward, although he had a lookout at the main top-mast head.

This, gentlemen, is the full and circumstantial account of the most lamentable and unforeseen catastrophe which it has ever been my misfortune to be concerned in. Lamentable on account of the loss which occurred, especially that of the captain, and unforeseen, as no one could have foreseen or fancied an accident of this description happening to a vessel so strongly built and so well bulkheaded as the *Cathedral*.

I send you below a full list of the names of all those lost and saved, and will forward to you on the first opportunity a detailed account of the captain's last illness, and other little matters here untouched, and have the honor to remain, gentlemen,

Your very obedient servant,
Andrew Richard Clarke
Late chief officer of the ship *Cathedral*

To this account was appended the certification of D. J. Cox, "3d officer, Reuben R. Heriott, 4th do. Daniel Draine, carpenter." They attested fervently to "the courage and skill of the chief officer in all his exertions for the safety of the ship..." Yet, for reasons unfathomed, one of the most dramatic stories of the loss of the *Cathedral* was left untold. Perhaps Chief Officer Clarke did include it when he reported on the captain's last illness, "and other little matters here untouched..."

The *Cathedral* had, among her people, a stewardess, Ann K. Flaherty of St. John, New Brunswick, who had previously served with Captain Howard on the transatlantic runs. Stewardess Flaherty flatly refused to leave Captain Howard to his fate. It is possible to picture the scene as Chief Officer Clarke called her: when she came to the cabin window, she must have listened as Clarke begged her to join them in the boat. And, no doubt, behind her in the cabin, Captain Howard urged her to go while she could. But Ann Flaherty waved them off, preferring to join her captain in death. Clarke may have failed to report this in his first account to his employers because of a certain reticence, knowing that Captain Howard left a family in Watertown, Massachusetts, but the tale did become public.

For sheer unequivocal guts Ann Flaherty rates heroic laurels in one of the many sagas of the sea and the people who follow it. Almost on a par with her, if not equal, was the doctor, C. W. Kirkenthal of Trenton, New Jersey, a passenger. Faithful to his oath as a physician, the doctor lingered too long with the ailing captain to save himself. Seven others were also lost. The article went on to say:

> The *Cathedral* was a superior, oak-built ship of 1600 tons register, with three decks, and cost, when coppered, $125,000 ... At the time of the disaster, she had on board, 2300 tons of coal, one half of which belonged to the Pacific Mail Steamship Co., and the other half was on the ship's account. Upon her cargo or freight money there is no insurance: and the ship herself is insured for only $75,000.

One writer noted that the *Cathedral* was but one of many severe losses suffered by the Enoch Train Company. For Samuel Badger, it was his last venture in clippering; the era was coming to an end, and Badger was wise enough to know it.

# VII  *Daniel Moulton*

ONE OF THE LEAST APPRECIATED CLIPPER BUILDERS in the saga of Piscataqua ship-building has to be Daniel Moulton, a highly skilled shipwright who put two of the glamorous vessels in the water. Little is known about Daniel Moulton himself. His name first appears in a Portsmouth city directory in 1851, listed as a carpenter with a house at 60 Islington Street, corner of Salem Street. Apparently he practiced his trade at the various Piscataqua yards, going where there was demand for his services. Like Stephen Tobey, Daniel Moulton following the great American tradition of going into business for himself, taking with him thirty-nine of his fellow craftsmen. In December, 1853, it was reported:

> A joint stock company, organized here to built ships, have leased part of Noble's Island, near Tobey & Littlefield. Capital, 40 shares at $500, with half to be reserve and half paid down. The stockholders are nearly all mechanics and most have been employed at some period on the construction of ships.[1]

In April, 1854, a news item made it obvious that the new firm was in business:

> Mechanics Shipbuilding Company. — This company is composed of 40 industrious and enterprising mechanics of the various trades and occupations in building vessels.
> They have commenced building on Nobel's Island and have two new ships under construction; one of about 1,100 tons, which is under contract to Ichabod Goodwin, who is always willing to assist the enterprising and the industrious, The other ship is of 900 tons

of a good model for a carrying ship and is for sale. We feel assured that this company can and will build as good vessels as any shipbuilders on the river.[2]

It says much for Daniel Moulton's leadership qualities that his fellow craftsmen apparently made him their head man. At one point, he was held in such high esteem that he headed the Piscataqua Shipwrights Association. There are no records in the state capital to show that Moulton and his associates ever incorporated, so it is not known how many of them there were. However, one was Frank N. Dickson of Eliot who had learned the shipbuilding trade under Moulton. When civilian shipbuilding slackened, Dickson went to work on the Navy Yard, where he had a safe job because of his wife's indirect connection to the brewing empire of Frank Jones. Like Dickson, Moulton went to work on the Navy Yard, becoming part of the 2,100-man force brought on by the demands of the Civil War. Moulton sold his house on Islington Street in October, 1867, to Joseph H. Berry, a blacksmith, and disappeared from the city directories.[3] His death is not on record in City Hall, and there is no probate material on him.

However, Moulton and the Union Company, along with Portsmouth Shipbuilding Company, contributed five square-rigged vessels to the numbers launched on the Piscataqua. The non-clippers included the *Ladoga*, launched in 1854, and the first vessel Moulton and his colleagues put in the water. Then there was the *Henrietta Marcy*, 1856, named in honor of Daniel Marcy's first wife, Henrietta Priest Marcy.[4] The second *Rockingham*, 1858, was the last ship built by the Moulton organization. The *Rockingham* was destroyed by the CSS *Alabama*.

## Morning Glory

SPECIFICATIONS: *Tonnage, 1,119. Length, 182 feet; breadth, 36 feet; depth, 26 feet. Owners, Ichabod Goodwin, William L. Dwight, Jacob Wendell, all of Portsmouth; W. H. Goodwin, Boston.*

**V**ERY LITTLE IS KNOWN about the career of the *Morning Glory*. It is as shrouded in fog as was her launching on October 30, 1854. While no records are available, it is probable that Ichabod Goodwin helped in financing the *Morning Glory*, thus making it possible for the Union Company to put its first clipper in the water. *The Chronicle* reported that a "fine ship of about 1,000 tons, was launched on Monday about 8 o'clock from the yard of the Mechanics Union. The fog was so dense at the time of the launching that it was seen by only a few individuals. We understand the company will now bring business to a close. The shipyards in this city will do little work the coming winter except to finish such ships as are now commenced."[5]

*The Chronicle* quickly heard from Daniel Moulton that rumors of his company's demise were premature. However, it would seem as though *The Chronicle* was partly right. Although the *Star of Hope* was built and launched by the Union Company, Moulton's last two ships were under the auspices of the Portsmouth Shipbuilding Company. The newspaper's observation merely reflected the conditions of the day. The sun was slowly setting over the wide yardarms of the clippers. Only five more would be built on the Piscataqua. Various builders, including Moulton, would construct full-rigged ships, but there would be no more queens of the ocean.

The *Morning Glory* cleared Portsmouth on January 30, 1855, under Captain William H. Parsons, formerly commander of Captain Goodwin's *Hope Goodwin*. She was bound for New Orleans and the cotton trade to Havre. However, she was diverted, loaded at Mobile, and then went to Havre. From there, she was put into the tea trade with Calcutta. Once, in 1856, she put in to St. Helena, Napoleon Bonaparte's island of exile. Back in France, she was sent to Bordeaux to load for New Orleans, taking twenty-four days for the passage. Late in November she headed for Liverpool, carrying 3,123 bales of cotton; thirty-eight half bales; twenty-six barrels of lard oil; 126 tierces of lard. The *Morning Glory* was making a fairly good run when she enjoyed one of her moments of glory—off the coast of Ireland, she had to stand by the *Adriatic*, bound from Liverpool for New York, which had gone up on the rocks near Dungarvon. Three men drowned, but the rest were saved.[6]

Transatlantic trade was apparently her forte throughout the years prior to the Civil War. As the menace of Confederate raiders increased the nervousness of northern shippers, the owners sold her to a British firm in April, 1864, for £7,800.[7] She was renamed the *British Crown*, but what happened to her under the Union Jack is not known.

## Star of Hope

SPECIFICATIONS: *Tonnage, 1,198. Length, 191 feet; breadth, 36 feet; depth, 24 feet. Owners, Charles H. Coffin of Newburyport and B.B. Titcomb of Ipswich.*

IF THE *STAR OF HOPE* is judged by her ill-starred career, it might have been better if the owners had left her under her original name, *Saint Paul*, with the pious hope that the saint's heavenly mantle would protect her from harm. Coffin not only contracted for the *Saint Paul*, but he also bought the *Witch of the Wave* (II), which George Raynes & Son was building across the North Mill Pond. The *Saint Paul*, as she was still being called, was launched on October 27, 1855. Within a few days after her launch, Charles Canny, a youngster of about twelve, exercised a Portsmouth boy's right to play on or around ships. The *Saint Paul* had not yet been masted, and young Canny fell through a mast hole, fracturing his skull and breaking a leg. At first the boy was reported dead, but he apparently recovered. The mishap took place in the dimly lit betweendecks area, where he was playing with chums.[9] In November, the clipper became the *Star of Hope*, and a writer for *The Newburyport Herald* reported, taking a markedly tolerant view, considering *Star of Hope* had not been built on the Merrimack:

> We passed a few minutes on board her yesterday. She will compare favorably with our Merrimack-built ships. Capt. Abraham Somerby is to command her.

The following advertisement appeared in a New York paper, on December 8, 1855:

> It gives me much pleasure to certify that Mr. A.K.P. Dearing and his rigging gang have performed the run from Portsmouth to New York with me in the ship *Star of Hope* and I am happy to say that they, one and all, have performed their duty to my entire satisfaction and whoever hereafter should wish the same duty to be performed would find they could not do better than to procure the services of these men.
> 
> A. Somerby, In command
> of Ship *Star of Hope*
> I fully concur with the above.
> C. H. Coffin for the owner

The *Star of Hope* was chartered at New York to carry stores out to the U.S. Navy's Pacific Squadron, and cleared New York, January 6, 1856, for San Francisco. It was an unfortunate passage. April 14 she put

Star of Hope *on the beach near the Cape of Good Hope. National Maritime Museum, Greenwich, England, collection.*

into Montevideo, Uruguay, on fire. Captain Somerby and his crew fought the fire to the best of their means, but eventually it was decided to caulk down the hatches, and make a run for Montevideo, where the *Star of Hope* arrived, April 28. The strategem apparently had worked because when the hatches were opened there was great heat, but no fire. Nevertheless, her cargo had to be discharged so repairs could be made. She spent May, June and July being repaired, was reloaded in August, and reached San Francisco on December 7, eleven months after setting out.

The *Star of Hope*'s evil star was still high in the heavens in June 1861. On the 13th (not a Friday, incidentally), Captain Somerby had to abandon her near the Cape of Good Hope, while on a passage from Liverpool with a cargo of railroad materials.

# VIII  *The Pierces*

ELBRIDGE G. PIERCE WAS THE ONLY real outsider in the Piscataqua ship-building scene, a shipwright who came from a remote area, and thrived for a time on the river. Pierce, and various authorities spell the name as Pearce and Peirce, came to the Piscataqua from "down east." The first public notice of his presence appeared in *The Portsmouth Chronicle,* March 20, 1856:

> E. G. Pierce, late of Farmingdale, Maine, has leased Pierce Island for a shipyard and commenced operations preparatory to laying the keel of a ship of 1110 tons for Henry Hastings of Boston. Col. Pierce has permission to build a bridge near the Gardner estate to the island.

The news item sparks speculation on at least three points: (1) from what military experience did Elbridge G. Pierce derive the rank of colonel? (2) was he related to the Peirce family of Portsmouth and Boston, which had full ownership of Pierce Island? (3) what kind of a bridge structure, if any, did he build from in front of the Wentworth-Gardner House to the island?[1]

Elbridge G. Pierce was born in Middleborough, Massachusetts, in 1801. While still a boy, he moved to Maine with his father, a successful shipbuilder. Young Pierce learned the shipbuilding trade from his father, and after his parents' death, continued their business at various yards in the vicinity of the Kennebec River. As early as 1826 he was listed as a builder of vessels, none of any great size. In 1831 he built the *Florence* at Hallowell, and put other vessels in the water at Pittston and Farmingdale. The *Vesta* was built at Gardiner in 1848; the *Mary Wilder,* 213 tons, was built at Pittston the same year. The biggest to his credit was the *Geranium*, a two-masted square-rigger of 433 tons, built at Farmingdale in 1854.

Pierce Island had experienced some construction activity between 1850 and 1852, when the famed floating dry dock for the Navy Yard was fabricated there before being towed across the river. *The Chronicle* asked no questions, simply deeming the proposal a good one, since "This enterprise cannot fail to increase the value of real estate at the South End, as well as to add materially to the most expansive and valuable mechanical interests of the city."[2]

Pierce brought his son with him to begin the new venture, as his own father had done with him. Elbridge, Jr., was closely associated with his father in the two vessels they built on Pierce Island. After they built the *Harry Hastings*, a non-clipper, in 1858, they apparently ceased operations. The younger Pierce went south and worked in bridge construction. With the outbreak of the Civil War, he came back north, and joined the shipwright gang at the Navy Yard, along with his father. The latter continued in that line until 1873 when he retired. The younger Pierce became Portsmouth's postmaster on April 21, 1869, a post he held until 1885 when a Democratic president took office. *The Chronicle*, a Republican-minded newspaper, described him as "the most efficient and popular postmaster the City ever had." After being turned out of office, young Pierce worked as superintendent for the Boston & Hingham Steamboat Company for a while before again going south to work as a railroad superintendent. When he returned, he was in ill health and died.

After his retirement from the Navy Yard, Elbridge Pierce, Sr., continued to live on Islington Street, but was spending the winter in Washington, D.C. with a daughter when he died on January 5, 1885. In his obituary it was noted that he had been a Free Soiler in his political beliefs, and became one of the first to join the Republican Party when it was formed in the middle 1850s. Pierce and his wife lived together for sixty years, and were the parents of four sons and three daughters. Three of the sons, Elbridge, George and Edwin, along with a brother, Captain Eben Pierce, were his bearers.

# Charger

*SPECIFICATIONS: Extreme clipper. Tonnage, 1,169. Length, 190 feet; breadth, 38 feet; depth, 23. Owner, Henry Hastings of Boston.*

ELBRIDGE G. PIERCE WASTED LITTLE TIME in beginning construction of his first Piscataqua vessel. Her keel was laid in late March or April, and she was launched on October 25, 1856. Those familiar with the swirling, tricky waters of the Piscataqua River off Pierce Island, can easily imagine the problems that were rampant in just getting the *Charger* launched. It was first planned to put her in the water on October 22, but *The Chronicle* reported:

> The new ship again did not go off. We now hear it said that she is to be discharged from her fastenings at seven o'clock this morning. As this is the first launch from the new yard, considerable interest is felt to see it. The ways are long, and no doubt the sight will be worth going to.

Before they did get *Charger* into the water, two of the caulkers were in an accident when staging outside the ship collapsed. They dropped nineteen feet to the ground. Benjamin Bailey escaped injury, Richard Waldron was severely jammed and bruised, "and we are informed has been delirious ever since the accident." Finally the *Charger* was launched. She did not clear the Piscataqua until December 9, arriving in Boston the eleventh and immediately attracting comment from *The Boston Journal*:

> The beautiful clipper ship *Charger* arrived in Boston Thursday from Portsmouth, N.H. She is 1,400 tons and was built by E.G. Pierce for Henry Hastings et al of Boston. She is said to be the best and most costly merchant ship of her size ever built in the United States. Capt. Charles Pearson, underwriters' agent, superintended her construction. She is to be commanded by Capt. Luther Hurd of New Orleans, who is part owner. We think her well worthy of a visit from all lovers of good ships.

The *Charger* cleared Boston for San Francisco early in January, 1857. It was a tribute to the business acumen of Henry Hastings that she was able to find a cargo so quickly. Shipping volume was declining, as the West Coast markets were becoming satiated, and also more self-sufficient. A commentary in March 1857, is to the point:

*Charger* sailing card promoting voyage to California.
*Bostonian Society, Boston, collection.*

> There are 135 first-class ships, averaging 1,000 tons each, now lying at the Chinca Island, waiting for cargoes of guano. Probably no other port in the world can boast of so large a fleet of splendid ships.[3]

It is surprising that both *The Boston Journal* and *The Chronicle* failed to comment on the *Charger*'s lack of the customary figurehead. Instead, she carried a plain billet, but "her stern was ornamented with a carved, mounted charger in full career."[4]

The *Charger* took 124 days on that first passage to San Francisco, not particularly good time, especially in view of the run by the *Stag Hound*. The two clippers went out of Boston Harbor on January 4, both being towed by the *Enoch Train*. When the *Charger* arrived, she found that the *Stag Hound* had been in port sixteen days, although hung up for seven days off the California coast. The *Charger*'s next run to the West Coast took 121 days, and she made a laborious passage of 100 days from San Francisco to Calcutta. "But from that port to Boston she retrieved herself. Leaving the Sand Heads, Dec. 25, 1858, she reached Boston, March 19, 1859, a passage of 84 days which has been beaten only by the 81 days of *Witch of the Wave* and the 83 days of the *Beverly*, and equalled only by the *Staffordshire* and *Dashing Wave*."[5]

Captain Hurd relinquished command on arrival in Boston, and Captain James B. Hatch took the *Charger* to San Francisco in 124 days. After Hatch, Captain J.N. Knowles took her out of Boston in March 1865. She had been advertised to sail on February 4, with the blurb: "This ship is well known to the trade for her short passages and for the fine order in which she delivers her cargoes.—She will sail as above, and Shippers will oblige by the prompt delivery of their engagements."

In March, 1869, under Captain William Lester, she came into New York with the most valuable cargo of teas yet brought to the United States. The total value was set at $1.7 million, and "every ounce of cargo was discharged in perfect order."[6] The *Charger* continued her dependable service for another five years. Finally, on December 14, 1874, she went on a reef, ten miles from Cebu, Philippine Islands. The wreck was sold for $7,595, and her then commander, Captain Creelman, was able to save part of the cargo of hemp. Henry Hastings had a second *Charger* built in Boston, and Captain Creelman was given command of her.

After the *Charger* only one more clipper, the *Shooting Star*, whose story has already been told, would be launched on the Piscataqua. A classic era in shipbuilding had come to an end.

# Notes

## Chapter 1

1. The *Simla* was a square-rigger, as big as many of the clippers, but not of that hull design.
2. *Baltimore Clipper*, p. 1.
3. *They Came to Fish*, vol. I, p. 105.
4. *American Clippers*, vol. I, p. v.
5. *Chronicle*, Feb. 11, 1853.
6. *Journal*, Oct. 18, 1850.
7. *Chronicle*, Oct. 19, 1886.

## Chapter 2

1. *Heyday*, p. 8.
2. *Chronicle*, Oct. 19, 1886.
3. Ibid.
4. Rockingham Deeds, vol. 267, p. 258.
5. Portsmouth Historic, p. 49.
6. Rockingham Deeds, vol. 288, p. 441.
7. *Chronicle*, October 19, 1886.
8. Ibid., March 23, 1889.
9. Ibid., April 3, 1899.
10. Ibid., March 3, 1860.
11. Ibid., May 28, 1853.
12. This clipper and the tug *R. B. Forbes* were named for a prominent Boston merchant, Robert Bennet Forbes, who made two different fortunes as a factor in the China trade.

13. *Chronicle*, Dec. 20, 1853.
14. *Greyhounds*, p. 197.
15. *Portsmouth Journal*, Nov. 23, 1850.
16. *Greyhounds*, p. 158.
17. *Chronicle*, Jan. 19, 1853.
18. Bayard Taylor was a world traveler, poet and lecturer.
19. *American Clipper Ships*, p. 568.
20. *Portsmouth Herald*, April 13, 1939.
21. *American Clipper Ships*, p. 705.
22. *The Boston Atlas.*
23. *American Clipper Ships*, p. 706.
24. *Greyhounds*, p. 213.
25. *American Clipper Ships*, p. 706.
26. Ibid.
27. Ibid., p. 707.
28. *Chronicle*, Sept. 28, 1865.
29. Ibid.
30. *Clipper Ship Era.*
31. Preston's apothecary shop was in the old Congress Block. He later had a manufactory on Bow Street.
32. *Portsmouth Journal*, May 8, 1852.
33. *Chronicle*, Dec. 10, 1852.
34. Ibid., Oct. 18, 1853.
35. *Greyhounds*, p. 234.
36. *Chronicle*, Nov. 26, 1852.
37. *Greyhounds*, p. 324.
38. *Chronicle*, Jan. 4, 1853.
39. *Chronicle*, May, 1855.
40. *Rockingham Messenger.*
41. *Chronicle*, May 1, 1856.
42. *Granite State Monthly*, vol. 6, p. 382.
43. *Chronicle*, Sept. 27, 1872.
44. Marine History of Pacific Northwest, p. 229.
45. *Chronicle*, Oct. 4, 1888.
46. Ibid., March 26, 1856.
47. Ibid., May 10, 1856.
48. *Greyhounds*, p. 342.

## Chapter 3

1. As a matter of fact, *Harriet Rockwell* did run up on the bank of Pierce Island on launching, as related in a news item in *The Chronicle*, March, 29, 1888. The ways were so sharp that *Harriet Rockwell*'s slide to the water could not be checked.
2. Exactly what John Mugridge built in the yard is not known. The registry of Piscataqua vessels between 1800 and 1860 does not

mention him as a builder, but he may have been Fernald's chief shipwright.
3. Charles Raynes was an eccentric brother of George Raynes. Charles built models for his brother.
4. *Heyday*, p. 49.
5. *Chronicle*, July 28, 1891.
6. *Heyday*, p. 25.
7. Ibid., p. 24.
8. Ibid., p. 62.
9. Ibid., p. 63.
10. *Portsmouth Journal*, March 15, 1851.
11. *Heyday*, p. 64.
12. Scrapbook, in author's possession.
13. *Heyday*, p. 65.
14. *The San Francisco Herald*, July 16, 1853; reprinted by *The Portsmouth Chronicle*.
15. *Chronicle*, Jan. 27, 1857.
16. Ibid., March 7, 1864.
17. Ibid., July 16, 1879.
18. Ibid., Oct. 28, 1852.
19. Ibid., Nov. 17, 1852.
20. *American Clippers*, p. 517.
21. Ibid.
22. Frederick W. Fernald's probate records show Samuel Badger as one of the appraisers of his estate.
23. *Chronicle*, May 7, 1853.
24. Ibid.
25. Ibid., June 16, 1853.
26. Ibid., June 20, 1853.
27. *The Boston Atlas*, July 11, 1853.
28. *Passage Makers*, p. 41.
29. *Chronicle*, July 31, 1855.
30. Ibid., Aug. 31, 1853.
31. Ibid., Aug. 30, 1853.
32. *Heyday*, p. 86.
33. *American Clippers*, p. 118.
34. *Chronicle*, Dec. 12, 1883.
35. Ibid., April 24, 1884.
36. *List of Merchant Vessels*, 1886.
37. Some of the longevity of these ships might be traced to the fact they were seasoned with salt.
38. From the transcript of a tape in the San Francisco Maritime Museum.
39. *The Sea Chest*, a periodical of the Puget Sound Maritime Historical Museum.

40. *Chronicle*, Jan. 30, 1854.
41. Ibid., Oct. 6, 1863.
42. In the British yard where she was built, *Alabama* was originally designated as No. 290.
43. *Alabama Claims*, p. 15.
44. *Heyday*, p. 89.
45. Pride in regional products was often carried to extremes. For example, the only clipper built in Florida, the *Stephen R. Mallory*, was constructed entirely of mahogany. Probably it was done because mahogany was readily available in Key West where *Mallory* was built in 1856.
46. *Heyday*, p. 91.
47. Ibid., p. 92.
48. Franklin House burned in 1879.
49. *Heyday*, p. 97.
50. Ironically, Frederick W. Fernald rests for all eternity in Union Cemetery, diagonally just across the way from George Raynes.

## Chapter 4

1. *The Herald*, Dec. 31, 1900.
2. *Chronicle*, Nov. 25, 1886.
3. Ibid., Jan. 25, 1864.
4. Ibid., June 23, 1866.
5. *Passage Makers*, p. 462.
6. *Rockingham Messenger*, June, 1854.
7. *American Clippers*, p. 574.
8. *Chronicle*, June 26, 1855.
9. Trial transcript.
10. Ibid., p. 154.
11. A copy of this transcript was presented to the Portsmouth Athenaeum many years ago by the Penhallow family.
12. *Chronicle*, May 27, 1862.
13. *Passage Makers*,
14. *Chronicle*, Jan. 20, 1855.
15. Ibid., March 4, 1856.
16. Ibid., March 3, 1884.

## Chapter 5

1. *Old Eliot*, vol. 2, January, 1898, p. 1.
2. *Granite State Monthly*,
3. Green Acre is the site of the Baha'i School. No trace of the Hanscom shipyard remains.
4. Old Eliot, p. 2.
5. *Merchant Sail*, vol. 5, p. 3088.
6. *Portsmouth Journal*, June 28, 1851.

7. *Merchant Sail*, vol. 5, p. 3088.
8. The Hanscoms were in the practice of cutting oak for their vessels in the Durham-Dover area, and freighting it to their yards on gundelows.
9. Johnson's rope walk was on the South Mill Pond, below Portsmouth Hospital. In the early days of the Civil War, it was used to garrison troops.
10. Justin Hanscom put the knowledge acquired in his father's shipyard to good use. His first job in Portsmouth was as a clerk for Tobey & Littlefield.
11. *Merchant Sail*, vol. 5, p. 3089.
12. *Pacific Marine Review*. Bradley Collection.
13. The British gave slave runners, when they captured them, short shrift, quite often hanging the captains. Because of the political aspects American naval commanders had to pussyfoot around. Only one slaver captain was hanged, and that was late in the Civil War.
14. *Pacific Marine Review*.
15. Report No. 20, U.S. House, March 2, 1866.
16. *Pacific Marine Review*.
17. This information was made available through the efforts of U.S. Rep. Norman D'Amours in dealing with the Maritime Administration.

## Chapter 6

1. *N.H. Gazette*, March 2, 1830.
2. Tarbell, p. 12.
3. Ibid., p. 10.
4. Tarbell says, p. 13, that Badger hired "a French immigrant" named J.M. deRochemont to tutor one of his sons in 1795.
5. *Chronicle*, Aug. 3, 1888.
6. Tarbell, p. 13.
7. Probate records, Alfred, Maine. (File No. 573.)
8. *Chronicle*, Aug. 3, 1888.
9. Named for a vessel built under its sheltering roof, the Franklin Shiphouse burned in 1935.
10. Probate records, Alfred, Maine. (File No. 572.)
11. *They Came to Fish*, Chapter 23.
12. *Chronicle*, May 19, 1886.
13. Ibid., Sept. 17, 1855.
14. There is also some indication that her owners received payment on claims against the *Alabama*, but the circumstances are not known.

## Chapter 7

1. *Chronicle.*
2. Ibid.
3. Ibid., Nov. 2, 1867.
4. Ibid., Nov. 4, 1893.
5. Ibid., Oct. 31, 1854.
6. Ibid., Dec. 27, 1856.
7. Ibid., April 19, 1864.
8. *Heyday*, p. 100.
9. *Chronicle*, Oct. 29, 1855.

## Chapter 8

1. Probably the earliest bridge to Pierce Island was of the pontoon type to facilitate movement of troops.
2. March 25, 1856.
3. *Chronicle.*
4. *American Clippers*, p. 82.
5. Ibid., p. 83.
6. *Chronicle*, March 20, 1869.

# Bibliography

## Books

Brighton, Ray. *They Came to Fish*. Portsmouth: Portsmouth 350, 1973.
Chapelle, Howard I. *The Baltimore Clipper*. Salem, Mass.: The Marine Research Committee, 1930. *The Search for Speed Under Sail*. New York: W.W. Norton & Co., 1967.
Cook, Adrian. *The Alabama Claims*. Ithaca, N.Y.: Cornell University Press, 1975.
Cutler, Carl C. *Greyhounds of the Sea*. New York: Halcyon House, 1930.
   *Queens of the Western Ocean*. Annapolis: U.S. Naval Institute, 1961.
Hackett, Frank W. *The Geneva Awards Acts*. Boston: Little, Brown & Co., 1882.
Howe, Octavius C., and Frederick C. Matthews. *American Clipper Ships*. Salem, Mass.: 2 volumes, Marine Research Society, 1926.
Lubbock, Basil. *The China Clippers*. Glasgow: Brown, Son & Ferguson, Ltd., 1957.
Pickett, Gertrude M. *Portsmouth's Heyday in Shipbuilding*. Newcastle: J.G. Sawtelle, 1979.
Stammers, Michael K. *The Passage Makers*. Brighton, Sussex, England: Teredo Books, Ltd., 1978.

## General References

Portsmouth City Directories.
*Vessels Built and Registered in Portsmouth — 1800-1860.*
*List of Merchant Vessels of the U.S.*, Treasury Dept. Document 875
Bureau of Navigation, 1886.
*Dictionary of American Biography.*
*Dictionary of National Biography.*

## Newspapers and Magazines

*The Portsmouth Chronicle.*
*The Portsmouth Journal of Literature and Politics.*
*The Portsmouth Herald.*
*The Boston Atlas.*
*The New Hampshire Gazette.*
*The Rockingham Messenger.*
*The Sea Chest.*
*The Granite State Monthly.*
*The Portsmouth Weekly.*
*The Portsmouth Times.*

## Pamphlets

*Old Eliot*, Vol. 2, Eliot Maine.
*Newcomen Address.* Edmund C. Tarbell, "William Badger," 1955.
*Penhallow Vs. Mersey Docks and Harbours Board*, a trial transcript, Marchant Singer & Co., London, 1860.

# *Index*

acceptance of clippers, 13, 39
*Achilles* (tug), 46
Ackerman, J.W., 92
*Active* (steamship), 104
*Adriatic* (ship), 152
*Alabama*, CSS, 59-61, 77, 97-99, 121, 151
*Alabama* Claims Commission, 99, 121
*Amazonas* (ship), 36
*Ambassador* (ship), 78
*America* (ship), 107
*America*, HBM, 12, 19, 136
American clippers, 11, 15
Andrews, General Joseph, 134
*Ann McKim* (ship), 13
*Ann Pitcairn Sharp* (bark), 148
*Annie Sise* (ship), 65
*Apollo* (ship), 141
*Arkwright* (ship), 63

Badger, Ann. *See* Neal, Ann Badger
Badger, Apphia, 141
Badger, Daniel, 142
Badger, David O., 139, 142
Badger, Ella E., 142
Badger, James M., 142
Badger, Lois, 141
Badger, Margaret, 141
Badger, Master. *See* Badger, William
Badger, Robert, 139

Badger, Samuel, 13, 14, 85, 137 (illus.), 139, 140, 141-142, 143, 145, 146, 149
Badger, Samuel A., 141-142
Badger, William, 68, 75, 136-141
Badger, William, Jr., 139, 140-141
Badger shipbuilders, 68, 136-149
Badger's Island, 68, 85, 122, 136-139, 140, 141
Bailey, Benjamin, 158
Baines & Company. *See* James Baines & Company
Baltimore Clipper, 12-13, 131
barge conversion, 95 (illus.)
bark conversion, 58, 61, 65, 93, 121
Barnum, P.T., 127
Bartlett, J.P., 120
Bartram, Captain John, 39, 40
*Bella Juana*. *See Wild Pigeon*
Berry, Joseph H., 151
*Beverly* (clipper), 161
Billings, Captain Samuel 145
Bingham & Reynolds, 58
Black Ball Line, 81, 112, 118, 119
blackbirding, 131
Boiling Rock, 63-64
Boston and Hingham Steamboat Company, 157
*Boston Argus, The*, 54-57
*Boston Atlas, The*, 27, 32-35, 39, 43-44, 111

Boston Cadet Band, 40
*Boston Chronicle, The*, 87
*Boston Journal, The*, 75, 127-128, 158, 161
*Boston Transcript, The*, 143
*Boston Traveller, The*, 45, 49
Bowen, Francis, 131-132
Boyd, Colonel George, 19-20
Bradford, William, 89
*Brenda* (schooner), 21
Brewster, Charles W., 40, 45, 73
Briard, Captain Charles F., 10 (illus.)
*Brilliant* (ship), 59, 61
*Bristol Packet* (ship), 139
*British Crown. See Morning Glory*
Brock, Captain, 104
Brown, Edmund M., 100
Bruce, L.A., 134
Buckingham, Captain, 32
Buttersworth, J.E., 51, 84

CSA. *See* Confederate States of America
*Cahoota* (ship), 103
California Gold Rush, 13-14
Canny, Charles, 154
cargoes, 15, 36, 58, 64, 92, 96, 161. *See also* China tea trade; Cotton trade; Guano trade
Carlton, Captain, 121
Castillo, Ramón, 36
Castle Island. *See* Badger's Island
*Cathedral* (clipper), 141, 146-149
*Catherine* (ship), 88
*Challenge* (clipper), 131
Chamber of Commerce, Greater Portsmouth, 15
Chapelle, Howard I., 12
*Charger* (clipper), 158-161 (illus.)
*Charger II* (clipper), 161
*Charlotte* (ship), 141
*Chickamauga*, CSS, 66
children's playground, 64, 104, 154
China tea trade, 13, 23, 77
*Chocorua* (ship), 22
Chonc Qua, 55, 57
*Chronicle, The. See Portsmouth Chronicle, The*
City Hotel, 54

*City of Manchester* (steamship), 117
Civil Service, 123
Civil War period, 59-61, 66, 77, 96, 97-99, 112, 118, 119, 121, 131-132, 151, 153, 157
Clark, Samuel, 145
Clarke, Andrew Richard, 146-149
*Climax* (clipper), 101
Coe, Joseph, 21, 117
*Coeur de Lion* (clipper), 54-58 (illus.), 65
Coffin, Charles H., 154
Coffin, Horatio, 100
Colonial period, 12
*Columbia* (ship), 68
*Columbus* (ship), 69, 73, 88
*Comet* (ship), 32
*Como* (ship), 65
Confederate States of America, 98
Connor, Captain, 92
*Constantine* (ship), 50
*Constitution*, USS, 70
Continental Navy, 136
Conway, Captain, 46
*Cossack* (schooner), 122
costliest Piscataqua-built clipper, 15, 127
costs analysis, building, 14, 127. *See also* Prices
Cottle, Thomas, 21
Cotton, Leonard, 100
cotton trade, 64
Coues, Samuel E., 140
Cox, D.J., 148
Crawford, Chief Officer, 58
Creelman, Captain, 161
crew shortage, 74-75, 96
Curtis, James O., 65
Cushing, Charles, 68
Cutler, Carl, 23-24, 35, 49, 65

*Daily Evening Telegraph, The*, 111
Dale, Captain Frank, 143, 144
*Danube* (ship), 23, 69, 73, 88
*Dashing Wave* (clipper), 57, 76, 85, 88-95 (illus.), 130, 161
Davis, J.E., 29
Davis, Jefferson, 98
Davis & Company, 130, 143

Dearing, A.K.P., 154
decline of clippers, 58, 65, 77, 103, 149, 152, 158-161
Dennett, William E., 139
Dennett's Island, 136
Derby, Mr., 40-41
design of clippers, 11-13
Dickson, Frank N., 151
Dockum, S.M., 134
Draine, Daniel, 148
Dwight, William L., 152

*Electra. See Witch of the Wave*
*Eliza* (schooner), 88, 107
*Elizabeth Hamilton* (ship), 123
Ellery, Captain, 53
Emerson ventilator, 111
*Emily* (brig), 19
*Emily Farnum* (clipper), 59-62 (illus.), 98
*Empire* (ship), 68
*Empire Egret. See Nightingale* (C2)
Empire Line, 134
*Empire State* (ship), 69, 73, 88
*Enoch Train* (tug), 146, 161
Enoch Train Company, 146, 149
Exchange Building Reading Room, 81
Exchequer Pleas, Court of, 116
*Express* (clipper), 61, 96-99

Farmer, Moses, 127
Farnham, B.F., 145
*Fashion* (ship), 88
fastest Piscataqua-built clipper, 78
Fernald, Frederick W., 14, 67-68, 69, 70, 103, 107, 127
Fernald, Samuel L., 15, 21, 46
Fernald, William D., 40
Fernald, William F., 22
Fernald, William L., 68
Fernald & Petigrew shipyard, 67-105, 130, 141
figureheads, 27, 32, 42, 50, 54, 86, 100, 111, 161
first Piscataqua-built clipper, 14
Fiske, Captain John D., 91, 130
Flaherty, Ann K., 149
*Fleetwood* (clipper), 141, 143-144
*Florence* (ship), 156

*Flying Cloud* (clipper), 16
*Flying Fish* (ship), 35-36
*Fortitude* (ship), 68
Foster, William H., 120-121
Foster's patent gear, 120, 121
Foulks, J.P., 82
*Fox* (ship), 13
Francis Lowe & Company, 111
*Franconia* (ship), 141
Franklin House, 100
Franklin Shiphouse, 141, 142
freight rates, 53
French, Daniel, 140
French, J.T., 145
Frost, Captain Charles, 97-98
Fry, William, 68
Funk & Wagnalls dictionary, 64

Gardner, George, 74
Gardner House. *See* Wentworth-Gardner House
*General Grant* (steamship), 107
*George Raynes* (ship), 50
George Raynes & Son, 14, 16-66, 67, 68, 154
*Geranium* (ship), 157
*Germania* (ship), 73
Gerry, Captain William B., 103
Gleason, William B., 100
Gleason & Sons. *See* S.W. Gleason & Sons
Glidden & Williams, 39, 108, 112, 115, 116
*Golden Gate* (ship), 32
Golden Gate bridge, 57
Goodwin, Captain Ichabod, 78, 88, 129, 130, 150, 152
Goodwin, W.H., 152
*Grace Darling* (clipper), 101
*Grace Darling* (steamship), 50
*Grandee* (ship), 107
*Granite State* (clipper), 73, 145
*Granite State II* (ship), 119, 142
Gray, Samuel, 100
*Great Republic* (clipper), 78
Green, Richard, 44
Green Acre, 122, 123
Gregory, Hugh McC., 29-31

Grinnel & Minturn Company, 27, 31
guano trade, 36, 58, 59, 64, 81, 87, 97, 104, 112, 115, 118, 119, 161
*Guiding Star. See Nightingale* (C2)
gundalows, 96, 103
Guthrie, Lieutenant John L., 131

Hackett, James, 136
Hackett, William H.Y., 22, 60, 88, 121, 145
Hadley, Josiah G., 146
Hale, Samuel, 68
half-clipper, 65
Hamilton, Captain A.G., 50, 53
Hammond family, 122
Hanscom, Isaiah, 123-124, 127
Hanscom, John (father of William), 122
Hanscom, John (son of William), 122
Hanscom, Justin V., 129
Hanscom, Master. *See* Hanscom, William
Hanscom, Samuel, 14, 122, 124, 127, 128, 129, 130, 134
Hanscom, Thomas, 122
Hanscom, William, 122-123, 124
Hanscom, William L., 122-123, 124
Hanscom shipbuilders, 122-135, 141
Hanson, Captain, 35 (illus.)
Hanson, N., 120
Harrat, Charles, 27, 40
*Harriet and Jesse* (brig), 19
*Harriet Rockwell* (ship), 67, 68
Harris, John, 118
*Harry Hastings* (ship), 157
Hastings, Henry, 100, 101, 103, 104, 156, 158, 161
Hastings, Walter, 103
Hatch, Albert R., 120
Hatch, Captain James B., 100, 161
*Henrietta Marcy* (ship), 151
*Henrietta Maria* (bark), 58
Henry, Captain, 105
Hepburn, Captain, 23
Heriott, Reuben R., 148
*Hibernia* (ship), 141
Hill & Carr, 120
Hoaglin, John, 62
*Hope Goodwin* (ship), 152
Hotchkiss, L.G., 65

*Howard* (ship), 141
Howard, Captain William H., 146, 149
Howland, Captain William, 27-28, 29, 30, 31
Hunter, Frank, 22
Hurd, Captain Luther, 158, 161
Huyche, Harold, 93

*Ida Raynes* (brig), 20
*Illustrated London News, The*, 44
*Indomitable. See Typhoon*
*Industry* (clipper), 65
*Isaac Boardman* (ship), 103

James Baines & Company, 81, 112, 119
Jameson, Captain William, 134, 135
*Janet Leach* (ship), 115
*Jean Ingelow* (ship), 22
Jenness, Richard, 59
Jimmy Ducks, 30
*John Land* (clipper), 101
*John Wade* (clipper), 130
Johnson, Jeremiah, 129
Jones, Frank, 129, 151
Jones, William, 59, 103
Jones & Company. *See* W. Jones & Company
*Josephine* (clipper), 134-135
Joy, A.T., 134
*Judah Touro* (ship), 69
*Judge Shaw* (clipper), 135
*Jumna* (ship), 65
Junkins, David, 21
Junkins, Isaac, 21
*Junta* (trawler), 105

*Kate Hastings* (bark), 100
Kell, Mr., 97
Kelley, Sir Fitzroy, 116
Kennard, Eleanor. *See* Raynes, Eleanor
Kennard, Nathaniel, 22
Kennard, Ruth Walker, 22
Key West Navy Yard, 132
*King of the Forest. See Sierra Nevada*
Kingsbury, Mr., 75
Kingsland, Daniel and Ambrose, 68-69, 70, 77, 107
Kirkenthal, C.W., 147, 149
Klondike Gold Rush, 93

Knight, Captain, E.D., 111
Knowles, Captain, J.N., 161
Knowlton, John, 75

*Ladoga* (ship), 151
Laighton, Dr. William, 64
Lancaster, Irene, 93-94
Lancaster, Captain Richard, 93-94
Lane, George, 22
Langdon, John, 136-139
Langdon's Island. *See* Badger's Island
largest Piscataqua-built clipper, 27
last Piscataqua-built clipper, 161
Lear, Tobias, 12
Lenholm, Captain Charles, 134
Less'Ard, Francis A., 57
Lester, Captain William, 161
*Levi Woodbury* (ship), 88
*Leviathan* (tug), 29
*Light Brigade* (ship), 119
Lind, Jenny, 127, 130
Lind, Mr., 30
Littlefield, Daniel, 14, 106, 107
Littlefield Lumber Company, 106, 107
*Live Yankee* (ship), 29
*Liverpool Times, The*, 74
Livius, Peter, 19
*London Shipping Gazette*, 44
*London Times, The*, 44
London World's Fair (1851), 127, 128-129, 130
longevity, 57, 88, 92-93, 95, 132-133
Lowe, John, 74
Lowe & Company. *See* Francis Lowe & Company
Lowrie, William, 81

Mackay & Baines company, 118, 119
*Maid of the Sea* (clipper), 65
*Mameluke* (ship), 29
Marcy, Captain Daniel, 15, 21, 69, 99, 100, 105, 142, 146, 151
Marcy, Henrietta Priest, 151
Marcy, Peter, 69, 98
Mare Island Navy Yard, 117
*Margaret Scott* (ship), 117
Market House, 63, 78, 93
Marryat's signals, 85
*Martha* (ship), 13
Martin, Martha J., 107

Martin, William, 40
*Mary M. Wood* (schooner), 123
*Mary Washington* (ship), 65
*Mary Wilder* (ship), 156-157
*Marysville Daily Appeal*, 104
Mason, John W., 42, 111
Mather, Captain Samuel W., 130-131
Mathes, J.F., 145
*Mayflower II* (ship), 12
Mayhew, Captain P.N., 36, 91-92
Mayo, Captain David D., 132
*McDonough* (schooner), 122
*McEllan* (schooner), 78
McGill, Thomas, 61-62
McKay, Donald, 16, 35-36, 78
McLean, Duncan, 57, 111
McNulty, Edward, 145
measuring criteria, 119
Mechanics Shipbuilding Company, 150, 151, 152
medium clipper, 23
*Mennon* (clipper), 65
*Mercantile Gazette*, 104
Merrimack-built ships, 154
Mersey Docks and Harbour Board, 116, 119
Meserve, Nathaniel, 19
Messenger, G.W., 103
*Midnight* (clipper), 100-102 (illus.), 103, 104
Miller, Ephraim, 39
Miller, Captain F.A., 127, 128, 129, 130
Miller, Frank, 63, 120
Miller, Captain Lewis F., 45
Millet, Captain J.H., 45
*Minna* (schooner), 21
Moran, Andrew, 64
Moran, John H., 64
*Morning Glory* (clipper), 152-153
*Morning Light* (Canadian-built ship), 112
*Morning Light* (clipper), 108-112 (illus.), 120
Morton, Mr., 92
Moulton, Daniel, 14, 150-155
Mugridge, John, 67, 68
Murray, Hannah, 19

Navigation, Bureau of, 105
navigational instruments, 62

Navy Yard. *See* Portsmouth Navy Yard
Neal, Ann Badger, 141
Neal, John, 141, 142, 145
Neal, William, 19, 20
Neal & Raynes shipyard, 20
*New Hampshire* (ship), 68
*New Hampshire Gazette, The*, 139
New Hampshire Port Authority, 15
*New York Express, The*, 74
*New York Herald, The*, 27-28
*New York Tribune, The*, 98
*Newburyport Herald, The*, 154
*Nightingale* (C2), 133
*Nightingale* (clipper), 15, 39, 65, 123, 124, 126 (illus.), 127-133 (illus.), 134
Noble's Island, 106, 150
*Noonday* (clipper), 103-105 (illus.)
Noonday Rock, 103, 104-105
*North Atlantic* (brig), 21
Northern Pacific Railroad, 62

oak wood, 100, 103
*Obed Baxter* (bark), 102
*Ocean Rover* (clipper), 10 (illus.), 120-121
Oliphant, David C. and Robert N., 23, 32
Oliphant & Son, 23, 46, 49, 50
*Orient* (ship), 50
ornamentation, 42, 43, 54-57, 73-74, 86, 100, 111, 129, 134. *See also* Figure-heads
ownership, 15

Pacific Mail Steamship Company, 77, 149
packet-type clipper, 39, 96
Palfrey family, 20
*Panama Star & Herald*, 146
Parker, Captain William, 59
Parrott, William F., 54, 58, 64
Parsons, Captain William H., 152
*Patrician* (ship), 105
Peabody Museum, 68
Pearce. *See* Pierce
Pearson, Captain Charles, 158
Peirce. *See* Pierce
Pendexter, George W., 145
Penhallow, Captain Pearce Wentworth, 115, 116-117, 118

Penzance, Lord. *See* Wilde, James Plaisted
*Peter Marcy* (ship), 69
Petigrew, Mary E., 99
Petigrew, William, 14, 67, 68, 69, 103, 105
*Phantom* (clipper), 117
Pickering, Captain McLauren F., 120-121
Pickering Street yard, 67, 105
Pickett, Gertrude, 16-19, 68, 91, 99, 103
Pierce, Captain Eben, 157
Pierce, Edwin, 157
Pierce, Elbridge, Jr., 157
Pierce, Elbridge G., 14, 156, 157, 158
Pierce, George, 157
Pierce Island, 14, 156, 157, 158
Pierce shipbuilders, 156-161
Pike, Captain Samuel W., 29
Piscataqua House, 146
Piscataqua Marine Laboratory, 67
Piscataqua Shipwrights Association, 151
*Planet* (brig), 19, 21, 50, 67
Plumer, Captain Washington, 85, 86, 87
*Polynesia* (clipper), 91
*Pontiff* (ship), 20
Pook, Samuel, 70, 123, 127
*Portsmouth* (ship), 136, 142
Portsmouth and South Berwick Ice Company, 96
Portsmouth Athenaeum, 12, 77, 81
*Portsmouth Chronicle, The*, 11-12, 14, 15, 46, 49, 50-53, 57-58, 63, 64, 76, 77, 78, 88, 92-93, 96, 98, 100-101, 103, 108, 120-121, 142, 143, 146-148, 152, 157, 158, 161
*Portsmouth City Directory*, 20, 145, 146
*Portsmouth Herald, The*, 100
*Portsmouth Journal, The*, 20, 40, 42, 44-45, 70-73, 74, 75, 129, 134
Portsmouth Lament, The, 41-42
Portsmouth Navy Yard, 14, 21, 22, 70, 85, 123, 136, 141, 142, 151, 157
Portsmouth Savings Bank, 59
Portsmouth Shipbuilding Company, 151, 152
*Portsmouth Weekly, The*, 101-102, 119
Preston, William R., 42, 100

prices, 36, 39, 61, 77, 100, 103, 112, 118, 121, 130, 132, 149, 153. *See also* Costs analysis
*Prima Donna* (clipper), 65
*Prince de Joinville* (ship), 46
privateers, 11, 12
*Progress. See Sea Serpent* (clipper)
prize master, 131–132
proportions, 67. *See also* Medium clipper
Putnam, Captain George W., 32–35
Putnam, Captain William O., 23, 78

*Queen of the Seas* (ship), 111
*Queen of the South. See Morning Light* (clipper)

*R.B. Forbes* (tug), 15, 23, 28, 40, 42, 54, 74, 100, 104, 108, 115, 143
*R.D. Shepherd* (ship), 69
*R.L. Myers* (schooner), 49
*Rainbow* (ship), 13
rake, 13
*Raleigh* (frigate), 136
Rand, Albert, 116
*Ranger* (frigate), 136
*Raven* (ship), 76
Raynes, Charles, 68, 107
Raynes, Eleanor Kennard, 20, 22
Raynes, Ellen, 20
Raynes, Emma, 20
Raynes, George, 13, 14, 16, 17 (illus.), 19–22, 23, 27–28, 32, 40, 44, 45, 50, 53, 54, 57, 63, 64, 67, 103, 107, 141, 143, 146
Raynes, George, Jr., 20, 21, 22, 63, 64, 65, 67, 107
Raynes, Ida, 20
Raynes, Nathaniel K., 20, 22
Raynes, William H., 20
Raynes & Fernald shipyard, 68, 141
Raynes & Son. *See* George Raynes & Son
Raynes Avenue, 16
Raynes Neck, 19
*Red Rover* (clipper), 23, 78–82 (illus.), 119
Reed, S.G., 65
Reed, Wade & Company, 65
reefing device, 120, 121
*Reindeer* (clipper), 23–24
*Relief* (pilot ship), 104

Remick, Jacob, 19
rerigging, 61. *See also* Bark conversion
Revolutionary period, 12, 19, 136
Richard the Lionhearted, 54
rigging, 111, 115, 120, 121
Rindge Shipyard, 19
Robert L. Taylor & Company, 78
Robinson, E.M., 65
*Rockingham* (ship), 61, 117
*Rockingham II* (ship), 151
Rockingham House, 73
*Roman. See William E. Roman*
*Rover. See Ocean Rover*
Rowell, Samuel, 100
*Royal Dane. See Sierra Nevada*
Royal Navy (British), 19
Russian-American Fur Company, 58
*Ruth. See Witch of the Wave*

S.W., Gleason & Sons, 68
sail plan, 115
*Saint Paul. See Star of Hope*
*Salem Register, The*, 39–41, 42
salt seasoning, 87
Salter, Captain Charles H., 74, 75–76, 77
Salter, John E., 103
*Samoset* (ship), 69, 93
Sampson & Tappan, 127
*San Francisco Call, The*, 92
*Santa Isabel. See Nightingale* (C2)
*Santee* (ship), 107
*Sarah Cowles. See Nightingale* (clipper)
*Saratoga*, USS, 131
schooners, 12
Scott, Thomas, 95
*Sea Serpent* (C2), 31
*Sea Serpent* (clipper), 14, 26 (illus.), 27–31, 32, 46, 50, 65, 78
*Sea Serpent Journal, The* (Gregory), 29
*Sea Witch* (ship), 76
Seddons, J., 77
Semmes, Captain Raphael, 59–61, 97–98
Sewall, Judge Samuel, 12
Sewall, Johnson & Company, 143
*Shackamaxon* (ship), 98
Shapley, Reuben, 122
Sharp, Captain Robert Claister, 148
Sheafe, John H., 145

Shelton, Thomas, 111
Shepherd, Mr., 69
Sherburne, Joseph, 140-141
*Shooting Star* (clipper), 65
*Shooting Star II* (clipper), 22, 61, 65-66, 161
Shreve, Captain Samuel V., 45
*Sierra Nevada* (clipper), 36, 76, 78, 91, 107, 114 (illus.), 115-119 (illus.), 120, 142
Simes, Captain Nathan Parker, 59-61
Simes, William, 145
*Simla* (ship), 11, 15, 107
Sise, Edward F., 74-75
slavers, 11, 131
smallest Piscataqua-built clipper, 23, 143
Somerby, Captain Abraham, 154, 155
specialization in trades, 21-22, 68
speeds, 12, 23, 28, 29, 32-36, 44, 45, 46, 49, 53, 57, 58, 64, 65, 74, 76, 77, 78, 81, 88, 91, 97, 100-101, 104, 111, 118, 130, 131, 143, 144, 161
Spence, John B., 60
*Staffordshire* (clipper), 45, 161
*Stag Hound* (clipper), 161
*Star of Erin* (ship), 98
*Star of Hope* (clipper), 152, 154-155 (illus.)
*Star of Peace* (clipper), 65
steamships, 70
Stephen Tilton Company, 88
Stewart, J.A., 95
Stoddert, Benjamin, 136
*Stornaway* (ship), 81
*Stranger. See Wild Duck*
Sun Shipbuilding company, 31
*Surprise* (clipper), 27
Swasey, Benjamin B., 100
*Sweepstakes* (ship), 35-36
*Syren* (clipper), 88, 91

Tacoma Mill, 93, 95
Taku Canning Company, 95
Tall Ships, 11
Tarantino, Captain John, 105
Tarlton, J.N., 145
Tay, Captain Benjamin, 45
Taylor, Captain Alfred, 131
Taylor, Bayard, 29, 30, 31

Taylor, Joseph D., 23
Taylor, Stephen, 85
Taylor & Company. *See* Robert L. Taylor & Company
temperance, 63
*Thomas Perkins* (ship), 67-68
Thorndike, Captain, 29
Tilton, Stephen, 84
Tilton Company. *See* Stephen Tilton Company
*Tinqua* (clipper), 23, 29, 46-49 (illus.), 50, 143
Titcomb, B.B., 154
Titcomb & Coffin, 63, 64
Tobey, James, 107
Tobey, Samuel, 107
Tobey, Stephen, 14, 106, 107, 150
Tobey & Littlefield shipyard, 21, 91, 106-121, 150
tonnage, 50, 69, 119, 120
Touro, Judah, 69
Towle, J. Warren, 100
*Trade Wind* (ship), 32
Train, George Francis, 130
Train Company. *See* Enoch Train Company
Trask, G.D.S., 92
Treadwell, Samuel P., 100
treenails, 73
Trinity College (CT), 29
Trott, S. Amos, 134
trunnels. *See* Treenails
Tucker, Captain George W., 54, 57, 58, 101-102
Tucker family, 69
Twombley & Lamson, 39
*Typhoon* (clipper), 69, 70-77 (illus.), 78, 127


Uncle David. *See* Junkins, David
Union Cemetery, 16, 22 (illus.), 69 (illus.)
Union Company. *See* Mechanics Shipbuilding Company
United States Congress, 81, 99, 105, 132
United States Maritime Commission, 133
United States Navy, 61, 123, 132, 136, 154

Valentine, William, 145
*Venice* (ship), 74
*Vesta* (ship), 156
*Voladora. See Wild Pigeon*

W. Jones & Company, 59
Waldron, Richard, 158
Walker, Charles W., 40, 63, 93
Walker, Horton D., 145
Walsh, Patrick, 121
Walters, Samuel, 71, 77
War of 1812, 13
*Water Witch* (clipper), 84 (illus.), 85-87, 88, 91
*Weekly Ledger, The*, 93
Weeks, Captain Nathaniel G., 145
Weeks, Captain Thomas M., 96
Weeks, Mrs., 145
Wendell, Jacob, 152
Wendell, William G., 134-135
Wentworth-Gardner House, 156
Western Union Telegraph Company, 132
*Western World* (ship), 69, 73, 88
Westervelt shipyard, 35
*Westward-Ho* (clipper), 91
whipsawing, 22
White, Captain Jeremiah D., 29
Whitmore, Captain Jacob D., 29, 46, 49, 65
*Wild Duck* (clipper), 50-53 (illus.)
*Wild Pigeon* (clipper), 32-36 (illus.), 46, 50, 65, 78, 118
*Wild Rover* (clipper), 101
Wilde, James Plaisted, 116
Willey, Zebulon, 141
*William E. Roman* (clipper), 14, 21, 23-24, 27, 36
*William H. Marcy* (ship), 11-12
*William L. Marcy* (schooner), 105
*William Price* (brig), 23
Williams, Mr. (mate), 29
Williams, Mr. (pilot), 116
Wilson, James Norton, 21-22
Wilson, John, 40
Winsor, Captain, 29
*Witch of the Wave* (clipper), 38 (illus.), 39-45 (illus.), 46, 50, 76, 161
*Witch of the Wave II* (clipper), 63-64, 154

Wood, Charles A., 123
Woodman, John R., 104
World War II, 11, 31, 133

yacht-like clipper, 127
Yeaton, John, 103
Yorke, William, 109
Young, Captain, 91
*Young Australia. See Red Rover*

*Zaritza. See Coeur de Lion*